# Wildlife-
## Friendly Plants

# Wildlife-
## Friendly Plants

make your garden a haven for beneficial insects, amphibians and birds

ROSEMARY CREESER

Photography by Steve Wooster

FIREFLY BOOKS

# A FIREFLY BOOK

Published by Firefly Books Ltd. 2004

First printing

Publisher Cataloging-in-Publication Data (U.S.)
Creeser, Rosemary.
   Wildlife-friendly plants: make your garden a
haven for beneficial insects, amphibians and birds /
Rosemary Creeser; photography by Steve
Wooster. — 1st ed.
[144] p.: col. photos., maps ; cm.
Includes index.
Summary: Guide to choosing and caring for plants
that will attract and sustain wildlife, including a
directory of 95 plants describing their blooming
season, height, width, U.S. zones and beneficial
wildlife.

ISBN 1-55297-954-7
ISBN 1-55297-953-9 (pbk.)

1. Gardening to attract wildlife. 2. Wildlife
attracting. I. Wooster, Steve. II. Title.
639.9/2 dc 22   QL59.C74  2004

National Library of Canada Cataloguing in
Publication
Creeser, Rosemary, 1959-
         Wildlife-friendly plants : make your
garden a haven for beneficial insects, amphibians
and birds / Rosemary Creeser ; photography by
Steve Wooster.
Includes index.
ISBN 1-55297-954-7 (bound).--ISBN 1-55297-
953-9 (pbk.)
         1. Gardening to attract wildlife. I. Title.
QL59.C74 2004                 639.9'2
C2004-901691-1

Published in the United States in 2004 by
Firefly Books (U.S.) Inc.
P.O. Box 1338, Ellicott Station
Buffalo, New York 14205

Published in Canada in 2004 by
Firefly Books Ltd.
66 Leek Crescent
Richmond Hill, Ontario L4B 1H1

Jacket image copyright © David Murray

Reproduction by Classic Scan, Singapore
Printed and bound by Imago Productions,
Singapore

# CONTENTS

# Introduction

In recent years I've planted a window box outside my first-floor apartment in central London with a selection of wildlife-friendly herbs, nectar-rich perennials, and trailing vines. As well as the enjoyment I've had watching beautiful pollinating insects close-up, it is satisfying to see firsthand that even the smallest of backyard habitats like this can play a vital role in sustaining wildlife throughout the year.

For too long wildlife gardening books have tended to focus on people who garden in rural areas, where there is sufficient space to plant large trees and hedges. But there is evidence that small suburban and inner-city spaces can also help to support diminishing populations of wildlife, by replacing some of the native habitats that have been lost from the countryside. In New York, the patchwork of community gardens created from barren, litter-strewn parking lots has become a haven for songbirds. In one of the larger gardens, the Clinton Community Garden, there have been sightings of more than 50 species of birds, several of which are now rare in the wild.

If you have a small vegetable garden or fruit trees, including plants that will attract pollinating insects is essential. Although some edible crops, like tomatoes and lettuce, are self-pollinated, others, such as runner beans and squash, rely on insects to pollinate them. The plant directory will help you to choose the nectar-rich plants that are favored by pollinators, such as bees and flower flies. With honeybee populations threatened by the *Varroa* mite, gardeners are being encouraged to attract alternative species of bee as pollinators of edible crops. One way of doing this is to grow plants like the lily-of-the valley shrub (*Pieris japonica*) that bloom early in the year, when solitary bees, like the red mason bee, are most active.

Planting wildlife-friendly perennials like bee balm can provide you with hours of enjoyment, allowing you to watch the extra beneficial insects and songbirds that they attract into your garden.

To help pollinate homegrown vegetables like these scarlet-flowered runner beans, it's a good idea to grow nectar-rich plants alongside so that they will attract bees.

Many wildlife-friendly plants are magnets for the "good bugs" (lacewings, ladybugs, flower flies) that can help you to control common garden pests, without using chemical sprays. The developing larvae of these beneficial insects often have particularly voracious appetites. A ladybug larva can eat between 30 and 40 aphids a day, while a single lacewing devours between 1,000 and 10,000 aphids in its lifetime. As the range of pesticides available for domestic use is reduced, gardeners are likely to become more reliant on methods of natural pest control such as these in the future.

Several of the plants featured in this book bloom exclusively at night, attracting moths and other night-flying pollinators. Because most night-blooming plants have white or pastel-colored flowers that reflect the moonlight, they can be used to create an unusual nocturnal garden that comes alive after dark. Exponents of this style of "moonlight garden" maintain that it is a great way to observe wildlife undistracted, when the daytime commitments to work, family and community have been met.

During the summer months the tightly packed heads of teasel (*Dipsacus fullonum*) attract flower flies. Flower fly larvae are one of the organic gardener's best friends because they consume large numbers of aphids over a long period of time.

# CHOOSING WILDLIFE-FRIENDLY PLANTS

# Choosing wildlife-friendly plants

By following a few simple guidelines you can create a space for wildlife, whether your garden is in the town or country. Wherever possible, plant native species. Because they have adapted to cope with local soils and conditions, they generally support a broader range of wildlife than introduced plants. Native plants are more likely to provide the specific mix of foods that native birds require and at just the time they are needed. For example, the fat-packed fruits of flowering dogwood (*Cornus florida*) help to fuel the long journeys that many migratory North American songbirds undertake in fall.

When you are choosing non-native plants steer clear of fast-growing alien plants, such as Japanese honeysuckle (*Lonicera japonica*), which sometimes overwhelm less vigorous indigenous species. In the past, fast-growing species like this have been mistakenly endorsed for their benefits to wildlife. The rapid dispersal of seeds by birds has allowed this rampant alien vine to colonize vast areas of Eastern United States. Communities of native plants have been crowded out and the range of foods available to birds much reduced.

Include evergreen shrubs and vines, which provide year-round structure and screen unsightly garden features, as well as sheltering wildlife. Grow semi-evergreen or evergreen varieties of

This single-flowered Oriental poppy has open, cup-shaped flowers that offer easy access to pollinating insects.

marginal plants for a wildlife pond or stream to provide refuge for amphibians and small birds.

It is also important to select plants that are compatible with the soil type, aspect, and site conditions found in your garden. You can use the Directory to determine this. If your soil does not have the recommended level of pH, consider growing plants in large containers filled with amended soil mix.

Borders planted with bold drifts of predominantly blue, purple, yellow or white flowers, are a magnet for butterflies and bees.

## Alluring flower colors, scents and shapes

Understanding the likes and dislikes of the creatures you wish to attract will help you choose appropriate plants. Like humans, insects and birds show preferences for particular colors of flowers and fruit. Many pollinating insects, like bees, are drawn to purple, blue, yellow, or white, and flowers from this end of the color spectrum often have markings in contrasting colors or unusual patterns to direct insects to the nectar and pollen. Some of these markings are visible to us — the maroon-spotted nectar guides inside foxglove blooms are a good example — but others such as the black-eyed Susan (*Rudbeckia hirta*) use ultraviolet pigments that the human eye cannot see. Most birds have a clearly developed color vision and tend to be attracted to plants with brightly colored fruits.

---

### The good bugs' favorite flowers

Lacewings, ladybugs, flower flies and parasitic mini-wasps find these plants particularly alluring.

**Dill** (*Anethum graveolens*)
**Korean angelica** (*Angelica gigas*)
**Pot marigold** (*Calendula officinalis*)
**Coriander** (*Coriandrum sativum*)
**Cosmos** (*Cosmos bipinnatus*)
**Poached egg plant** (*Limnanthes douglasii*)
**Goldenrod** (*Solidago*)
**French marigold** (*Tagetes patula*)

---

those with a heavy or spicy fragrance. If you want to attract nocturnal moths, concentrate on night-blooming plants, like evening primrose (*Oenothera*) and night-scented stock (*Matthiola*

Yellow, orange and white flowers, like this poached egg plant (*Limnanthes douglasii*) are a favorite of flower flies.

The umbrella-like flowers of this dill (*Anethum graveolens* 'Dukat') provide a landing pad for small beneficial insects.

Bees have good color vision but although they find the ultraviolet part of the color spectrum particularly alluring, they are "red blind" and tend to ignore red flowers. However, contrary to expectations, bees can see the red field poppy (*Papaver rhoeas*) because its petals reflect ultraviolet light. Butterflies are generally attracted to flowers with strong colors. The brilliant orange-red butterfly weed (*Asclepias tuberosa*) is a good example of this.

Scent is another important feature that plants employ to attract pollinating insects. Bees tend to favor plants with delicate or sweetly scented flowers, whereas butterflies are often drawn to

*longipetala* subsp. *bicornis*), which give off a strong or sweetly scented perfume after dark.

Plant the traditional single-flowered forms or cultivars — many double-flowered hybrids are sterile and of little use to pollinating insects. The shape or arrangement of the flowers is also an important factor. Dill (*Anethum graveolens*) and Queen Anne's lace (*Daucus carota*) bear flowers in umbels. These and plants such as sunflowers (*Helianthus annus*) present perfect landing platforms for small insects, and copious tiny blooms on which to feed. Their nectar is easily reached by insects with short tongues, such as flower flies, parasitic mini-wasps and beetles.

### Selecting a small tree or shrub

Most forest trees recommended for their benefits to wildlife are too large for the average garden, but many small species offer safe nesting places, shelter and food. The trees included in the box below are small enough for the average garden, and will provide food for birds and pollinating insects, a place for birds to nest and insects to hibernate. Flowering dogwood (*Cornus florida*) is a great example — dozens of species of songbird obtain sustenance from its bright red fruits and the insects that shelter in its bark. Although dogwoods can grow 20 ft. high and 25 ft. wide (6 by 8 m), many popular cultivars are half this size and make ideal specimen trees for a small garden. If there's only space in your garden to plant a single tree, choose one that produces berries, nuts or seedpods. Deciduous species are generally more valuable than other varieties because they attract more insects and often provide food at different times of the year for pollinators, birds, and small mammals.

Try to choose a species that flowers in early spring or in fall when other sources of nectar are scarce. The Eastern redbud (*Cercis canadensis*), a small multistemmed tree, falls into this category. The purplish-pink, pea-like flowers that appear on its bare branches in spring provide nectar for many early-flying butterflies and bees. Before choosing a cultivated variety of tree or shrub investigate its hardiness, local suitability and fruit

The long-lasting golden-yellow crab apples of *Malus* 'Golden Hornet' provide winter food for birds, when other trees or shrubs have been divested of their fruit.

---

#### Small wildlife-friendly trees

Where space is limited, the following trees offer a source of shelter and food for many pollinating insects and songbirds.

Downy serviceberry (*Amelanchier arborea*)
Flowering dogweed (*Cornus florida*)
Cockspur thorn (*Crataegus crus-galli*)
'Sparkleberry' holly (*Ilex* 'Sparkleberry')
'Donald Wyman' Crab apple (*Malus* 'Donald Wyman')
'Colorata' Purple leaf-bird cherry (*Prunus padus* 'Colorata')
Stag's horn sumach (*Rhus typhina*)
Black elder (*Sambucus nigra*)
'Lutescens' Whitebeam (*Sorbus aria* 'Lutescens')

---

production. The hardy 'Royal White' Eastern redbud, for example, is particularly recommended for planting in northern gardens. It's worth remembering that types of trees and shrubs that produce abundant fruit will be more valuable to wildlife than less productive cultivars.

It is especially important to take into account the soil type, aspect, and conditions of the site for a new tree. Flowering crab apples (*Malus* spp.) grow well in almost any soil type but prefer open sunny sites. In partial shade the features that benefit wildlife are reduced — flowering is less profuse and the cherry-like fruits that provide food for birds are fewer and take longer to ripen.

If there's not enough space to plant a small tree choose one of the shrubs included in the Directory. Shrubs can provide shelter and safe travel routes for mammals and birds, particularly when they are planted in groups. They are also useful for enhancing the wildlife value of an area planted with mature trees, by creating an understory or lower layer of vegetation. As well as attractive flowers and fruit, several of the shrubs included have spiny thorns that offer nesting birds protection against predators. Because they mature relatively quickly, most shrubs will be of benefit to wildlife sooner than a slow-growing tree, which may take several generations to reach its ultimate height and spread.

### Wildlife-friendly plants for small spaces

It's perfectly possible to create a haven for wildlife if you garden in a small space, such as a courtyard or balcony. Although you won't have room for a large tree, there are plenty of ways to attract beneficial pollinating insects and birds. Many of the wildlife-friendly plants in the Directory have been selected because they are suitable for growing where space is limited. Compact shrubs, such as cultivars of *Pieris japonica* and flowering vines, like star jasmine (*Trachelospermum jasminoides*), will thrive in a large container if re-potted every third or fourth year. Trailing nasturtiums can be grown in a hanging basket, and the robust stems and reduced height of *Cosmos* 'Sonata White' will withstand the strong winds on roof gardens and balconies.

Choose plants for containers that will cope with short periods of drought. Herbs such as lavender, rosemary and thyme grow well in terracotta pots. Group the pots close to a pathway

In a small space it is especially important to choose containers that are harmonious with the hard landscaping.

or entrance so that you can watch butterflies and bees close-up and appreciate the plants' aroma when you brush past them. Grouping container-grown plants together in this way also makes them easier to water and helps to reduce evaporation during hot, dry spells.

For a roof garden or balcony, concentrate on plants that thrive in difficult environmental conditions. Alpines and coastal plants like thrift (*Armeria*) will tolerate extreme sunlight and strong winds. For a large roof terrace an evergreen hedge of *Elaeagnus* x *ebbingei* will act as a windbreak, providing food and shelter for insects and birds.

Before making a final decision check on the vigor and ultimate height and spread of the plant. Virginia creeper (*Parthenocissus henryana*) is ideal for small spaces because it is less rampant than other forms of this popular wildlife-friendly vine.

CREATING A HAVEN FOR WILDLIFE

# Creating a haven for wildlife

One of the main aims of a wildlife-friendly garden is to re-create some of the native habitats that have been lost from the countryside, including woodlands and forests, wetlands, hedgerows or thickets, and meadow, pasture and prairie lands. The best way of doing this is to work with the existing site conditions, exploiting what you already have, rather than fighting against it. Your garden will be more appealing to wildlife if you can incorporate a number of habitats, offering shade, shelter, water and food. Wherever possible, link the habitats together and provide corridors, such as hedges and areas of long grass, to encourage creatures to explore farther afield. Designing like this has advantages for natural pest control, as frogs are more likely to venture into different areas of the garden in search of slugs and insects.

## A wildlife pond

A small pond or water feature is probably the most important wildlife habitat you can include in your garden. If young children use it, cover the surface of the pond with a rigid metal mesh fixed to a wooden or metal frame to prevent accidents.

A wildlife pond should be situated in an open, partly sunny spot, away from overhanging trees. Include a shallow ledge as a planting platform, and gently sloping sides to allow safe access to and from the water for creatures that use the pond to drink and bathe. Grow aquatic plants, like watermint (*Mentha aquatica*), around the shallow margins, preferably on the south-facing side. As well as providing shelter for amphibians and small water bugs, this nectar-rich perennial will encourage butterflies to visit the pond.

## A mini woodland

Although few people will have the space to plant an entire forest, a carefully chosen tree can create the effect of a woodland edge, especially if the canopy is underplanted with a carpet of low-growing woodland edge plants. Multistemmed species, like the snowy mespilus (*Amelanchier lamarckii*) and red-osier dogwood (*Cornus stolonifera*), can be successfully coppiced by cutting all the branches down to ground level every third year. Coppicing is an old technique of managing woodlands, and it promotes strong growth, and superior foliage and stem color.

The densely planted margins of this wildlife pond will provide shelter for many amphibians and small water birds.

## A wildflower meadow

The cowslip (*Primula veris*) was once a common spring flower across Europe, but the reduction of old pastureland has led to a fall in colonies of this lovely wildflower. Although not native to North America, cowslip can be naturalized here by turning all or part of a poorly drained lawn into a wildflower spring meadow. Stop mowing the lawn in autumn, and start planting spring-flowering bulbs, like the snake's head fritillary (*Fritillaria meleagris*), and moisture-loving wildflowers, like the cowslip, ragged robin (*Lychnis flos-cuculi*) and wood anemone (*Anemone nemorosa*).

Use young plants that you have raised separately or bought. Seeds sown on the surface of an existing lawn will have a hard job competing with vigorous grass roots. Informal paths can be

Laurustinus (*Viburnum tinus*) flowers early in the year when many pollinating insects are starting to emerge from hibernation.

Aster x frikartii 'Mönch' offers a vital source of nectar for butterflies and bees preparing for winter.

mown into the meadow to allow access while retaining a natural feel. Spring meadows should be left uncut until early summer, when the foliage of the bulbs has died down and the flowers have reseeded. Rake off the mowings to maintain low soil fertility and to prevent grasses from engulfing other, less vigorous meadow plants.

## Providing year-round food

Try to design your garden so that it offers a more-or-less continuous succession of flowers to provide nectar and pollen throughout the year. This is particularly important for pollinators, like bumblebees, which need a constant supply of flowers in spring and summer. The symbols at the top of each page in the Directory section indicate the flowering season for each plant.

Include some nectar-rich plants that flower early or late in the year when alternative sources of nectar and pollen are scarce. Winter aconites (*Eranthis hyemalis*), for example, are one of the earliest spring-flowering bulbs. The bright yellow, buttercup-like flowers open on mild days in late winter and are a vital early source of nectar for bees emerging from hibernation. You can help to support migrating butterflies by growing perennials like gayfeather (*Liatris spicata*), shrubs such as the sweet pepper bush (*Clethra alnifolia*) and herbs like oregano (*Origanum*), whose nectar-rich blooms often linger until the first frosts.

### Nectar sources for emerging and over wintering insects

Try to include some nectar-rich plants that flower at the time when pollinating insects are emerging from or preparing for hibernation.

**Emerging insects**
Cornelian cherry (*Cornus mas*)
Tomasini's crocus (*Crocus tommasinianus*)
Winter aconites (*Eranthis hyemalis*)
Oregon grape (*Mahonia aquifolium*)
Laurustinus (*Viburnum tinus*)

**Overwintering insects**
Strawberry tree (*Arbutus unedo*)
Michaelmas daisy (*Aster x frikartii*)
Purple coneflower (*Echinacea purpurea*)
'Cloth of Gold' Goldenrod (*Solidago* 'Cloth of Gold')
Fragrant vibernum (*Viburnum farreri*)

Include a variety of plants that will provide songbirds with cover, a safe nesting site and nutritional food throughout the year. You could include a small tree, a berry-producing shrub, summer-blooming perennials that are left to go to seed, and a fruiting vine. Trees such as downy serviceberry (*Amelanchier arborea*), which has sweet fruits that ripen in late spring or early summer, supply the energy that songbirds need to rear their chicks. Many migratory songbirds will devour the fat-rich fruits of flowering dogwood *(Cornus florida)* and southern magnolia *(Magnolia grandiflora)* in preparation for the long journeys they undertake in fall. Where possible, include a tree or shrub with fruit that will persist through winter.

**Right plant, right place**
Siting plants is a crucial factor in determining whether they will be visited by beneficial wildlife. Nectar-rich plants growing in sunny, sheltered places are more likely to attract bees and butterflies than those growing in shaded or windy locations. Red valerian (*Centranthus ruber*) is a useful choice for hot, dry coastal gardens because it is drought-tolerant and has a long flowering period, but remember that bees are more likely to visit its tiny, honey-scented flowers if it is sited away from strong winds. On an exposed coastal site, create a wildlife-friendly windbreak of evergreen shrubs, such as *Elaeagnus x ebbingei* or the daisy bush (*Olearia macrodonta*), which tolerate salt-laden air.

Plant butterfly-attractants in groups rather than as single specimens, because butterflies

Nectar-rich plants growing in sunny, sheltered places are more likely to attract bees and butterflies than those growing in shaded or windy locations.

prefer to visit stands of brightly colored flowers. Also, try to arrange the tall plants toward the back of the border, with shorter ones at the front. This is because butterflies sometimes experience problems landing on flowers that are partly obscured, particularly when it's windy. Before they start to feed, butterflies like to bask in the early morning sunshine on sun-warmed paving or gravel paths. Planting a nectar-rich creeping thyme, like *Thymus polytrichus* subsp. *britannicus*, in the small crevices between the stones is sure to enhance their experience.

Most of the night-pollinated plants included in this book release a delicious fragrance as soon as light and temperature levels drop. The best position for them is close to a house entrance or outdoor seating area, where the scent of the flowers and the antics of night-flying insects can be appreciated at close quarters.

**A butterfly haven**
If butterflies are to be more than passing visitors, you'll need to include several plants on which their young feed. In the Directory a caterpillar icon indicates plants that provide food for

---

## Winter food for birds

These plants are particularly valuable in late winter when snow covering the ground prevents songbirds from finding insects and worms to eat.

Cockspur thorn (*Crataegus crus-galli*)
'Winter Red' winterberry (*Ilex verticillata* 'Winter Red')
'Donald Wyman' crab apple (*Malus* 'Donald Wyman')
'Mohave' firethorn (*Pyracantha* 'Mohave')
Stag's horn sumach (*Rhus typhina*)
Hedgehog rose (*Rosa rugosa*)
'Joseph Rock' mountain ash (*Sorbus* 'Joseph Rock')
*Viburnum trilobum* (syn. *V. opulus* var. *americanum*)
    (American cranberrybush)

caterpillars. Butterflies will extract nectar from a wide range of flowers, but most will lay their eggs only on specific types of plants. The Monarch butterfly, for example, will seek out a member of the milkweed family such as the butterfly weed (*Asclepias tuberosa*) to lay her eggs. Larval food plants are best grown in groups in a sheltered, sunny spot.

If you have the room, choose an inconspicuous but sunny area of lawn where the grass can be left uncut and allow a small patch of stinging nettles (*Urtica dioica*) to grow unfettered. Butterflies, such as the Fiery Skipper, prefer to lay eggs in long grass, and if nettles are grown in a sunny spot they will provide food for the caterpillars of some of the most common butterflies, including the Red Admiral, Painted Lady and Milbert's Tortoiseshell. If you have fruit trees, don't be over fastidious about clearing away windfalls, because some species of butterflies prefer to feed on rotting fruit. Try to provide a shallow, muddy puddle in a sunny spot. Many butterflies love to drink from mud puddles using them to obtain essential minerals and salts dissolved from the soil.

Avoid using chemical sprays to deal with insect pests and weeds. Even pesticides marketed as "wildlife-friendly" are unselective in their effects and will harm beneficial pollinators, including butterflies. There are many simple cultural methods for controlling insect pests (see page 31).

A patch of stinging nettles in a sunny spot will provide nourishment for several broods of caterpillars each year.

**Avoiding excessive tidiness**

If you want to provide shelter and food for wildlife try not to make your garden too tidy. Areas of long grass and piles of leaves, stones and twigs provide shelter for many beneficial insects and small mammals. Always check carefully for signs of life by gently turning over winter bonfires before igniting them. Woodpiles are also valuable for birds, which will search among the branches for insects and use small twigs to build their nests.

Woodpiles provide food and shelter for many insects and invertebrates, such as stag beetles, while fallen leaves, left on the bare ground beneath trees and shrubs, are beneficial for wildlife.

# HOW TO PLANT

# How to plant

There is an old saying among gardeners that for every cent you spend on the plant you should spend a dollar on the planting hole. It is certainly true that if you spend a little time and money providing plants with the best start in life they are more likely to thrive.

Before planting check the Directory to see if you have chosen the right position and if there is enough space for the plant to reach its mature height and spread. This is particularly important with specimen trees that may prove difficult to move once established. Most herbaceous perennials can be moved, but some, like giant sea kale (*Crambe cordifolia*), develop a deep taproot that makes them hard to transplant. In a wildlife-friendly garden there is a strong case for keeping the amount of replanting to a minimum because of the disturbance it causes to beneficial insects, such as ground beetles, which live on or below the surface of the soil.

## Soil preparation

Once you have decided where you are going to plant, clear the area of perennial weeds. This is crucial, because they will compete with your plants for nutrients and water.

The best way is to fork over a small area at a time, loosening the soil around the roots, and then go over the ground by hand, removing every last piece of weed. Try not to leave even small portions of the roots underground, because the weeds will soon regenerate. Clearing the ground usually brings annual weed seeds to the surface of the soil to germinate. They are relatively simple to remove by hand while they are young. Annual weeds can be composted, but perennial weeds should be bagged up or burned.

When the planting area is weed free, break up large clods of earth and remove large stones. Rake over and firm the soil with a metal rake until any remaining clods are broken down and the planting area is level. Next, broadcast a balanced slow-release fertilizer evenly across the surface of the soil, at the rate recommended on the packaging, and rake in well. If you are sowing seeds directly in the ground, make sure it does not have small dips where moisture may collect, causing them to rot. The soil in a seedbed needs to be the consistency of fine breadcrumbs so that fine, hair-like roots can easily permeate it. Thoroughly soak the rootball of woody and herbaceous plants before planting.

## Planting a climber

1 Plant climbers at least 18 in. (45 cm) away from a wall so they are not shielded from the rain. Do not remove the central cane because it provides support for the stems when planting.

2 Position the climber in the center of the hole at a 45 degree angle towards the support. Use a bamboo cane placed across the surface of the soil to check the planting depth.

## Planting a climber

Hardy climbers such as English ivy (*Hedera helix*) can be planted at almost any time of the year, as long as conditions are favorable. Vines such as star jasmine (*Trachelospermum jasminoides*) that are not totally hardy, should be planted in spring so that they have time to become established before the onset of winter. Climbing plants need a wooden trellis, netting or framework of galvanized wires to support and encourage them to climb. Make sure that the structure is large and strong enough to support the mature plant. So that air can circulate freely, fix trellis to a framework of battens, or use vine eyes that allow wires to be held about 2 in. (5 cm) from the surface of the masonry.

## Planting a micro-habitat

If you have only a tiny outdoor space it is still possible to create a small-scale wildlife habitat such as a micro meadow, or a mini pond or bog garden in a large pot. With a little preparation a wooden half-barrel makes an ideal pool and provides a bigger planting area than most glazed terracotta containers. A large plastic pot is another option. Some of the newer designs are lightweight, stylish copies of those using more costly traditional materials, such as stone. Move the empty container to the chosen site — it will be too heavy to move once it is full of water and planted.

Make sure that you select a suitable planting medium. Most meadow flowers will flourish in

When creating a mini pond, choose compact, non-invasive species, such as pygmy water lilies (*Nymphaea* 'Pygmaea Helvola' and *N.* 'Pygmaea Rubra').

peat-free soil mix, to which a little Perlite or horticultural grit has been added to improve drainage. Bog plants prefer a rich loam-based mix, while marginal and deep-water plants are best grown in a special aquatic compost, which is low in nutrients. It is important to select plants of similar vigor. Some marginal and bog plants are vigorous or have large leaves that make underplanting difficult. If they are grown together in a container, they will quickly overwhelm other, less vigorous plants. One alternative is to group together vigorous or large-leaved species such as white skunk cabbage (*Lysichiton camtschatcensis*) in separate large pots to create an attractive display.

3 After backfilling the hole, use your heel to firm the soil around the plant to make sure that no air pockets remain.

4 After planting, select three or four of the strongest stems; arrange into a fan shape and tie each to a separate bamboo cane. Leave the canes until the stems have reached the support.

## Watering

If they are to flourish, all plants need an adequate and regular supply of water. Container-grown specimens and new plantings have the greatest need, but even established plants need to be watered every 10 days or more often during dry spells. To encourage new plants to develop deep roots, enough water should be applied so that it can soak the soil, rather than merely wetting the surface. It is best to water at ground level in the morning, directing the water toward the base of plants, rather than soaking the foliage and flowers from above. Not only is this more efficient — much of the water delivered by overhead sprinklers evaporates or is blown off-course — but it is also less likely to provide the conditions that encourage pests and diseases. Using a porous hose that allows water to seep slowly into the soil through a network of tiny holes is a comparatively low-cost option. The hose can either be moved around to where it is needed or buried at a depth of 4 to 6 in. (10 to 15 cm) as a permanent irrigation system.

## Water conservation

As a wildlife-friendly gardener there are several things you can do to conserve and make the best use of water. Modifying drainpipes so that rainwater is redirected to a rainbarrel is relatively easy using a down-pipe converter kit, available from most builders' merchants. Because rainwater has a low pH it is particularly suitable for watering plants like high-bush blueberries (*Vaccinium corymbosum*) that dislike alkaline conditions and for topping up the water in wildlife ponds. To keep children and mosquitoes out and to discourage evaporation and algal blooms, your rainbarrel should have a tightly fitted lid.

Container-grown plants tend to dry out in hot, sunny weather. Those in wide containers are most at risk, because evaporation from the surface of the soil is greater than from narrow, upright containers. Container plants are best grown in a loam-based soil mix, to which water-retaining granules and a slow-release fertilizer have been added when planting. The clay content of the soil mix helps to retain water and nutrients, and it is better than many types of loam-less mixes, which dry out quickly and are hard to re-wet. It is a good idea to cover the surface of containers with a

Decorative mulches are an attractive way of reducing water loss due to evaporation from the surface of containers. Try using seashells, either crushed or whole, obtained from a sustainable source.

decorative mulch. This helps to set off the plants, as well as reducing evaporation from the surface. If you are keen to use recycled materials, many sellers now offer a range of mulches made from crushed seashells, slate chippings, and even recycled compact discs!

Applying a 3 to 4 in. (7.5 to 10 cm) layer mulch of well-rotted garden compost, manure, leaf mold, cocoa shells or shredded bark after planting helps to retain moisture and inhibit the growth of annual weeds. Organic mulches break down slowly over time, adding nutrients to the soil and helping to improve its structure. Always soak the ground before mulching and leave a mulch-free area around the stems and crowns of the plant.

Plants grown high up on a roof garden are at particular risk of drying out, because of the combination of strong winds and intense sunlight. If you are creating a high-rise garden it is prudent

Automatic watering systems are ideal for plants on a roof garden that are at risk of drying out if they are not watered frequently.

to install an automatic irrigation system that delivers a regular, controlled supply of water. Most systems are timer-controlled and use a network of pipes to supply water at a pre-programmed time through a small outlet fixed in the top of the container. If you decide to install the system as a DIY project, try to conceal the connector pipes among the foliage or under a loose mulch, which reduces evaporation and is more aesthetically pleasing.

This soaker hose system will relieve you of routine watering as well as irrigate plants when you are away.

# ENCOURAGING AND SUSTAINING WILDLIFE

# Encouraging and sustaining wildlife

If you want to encourage and sustain wildlife, try to work more with nature. Given a little time it's possible to build a self-sustaining garden that will attract beneficial insects, amphibians and birds to help deal with insect pests. A wildlife-friendly garden will have a more natural appearance, but this does not mean that it has to look unkempt and overgrown.

One way of sustaining wildlife is to regularly deadhead flowering plants, by removing the spent flowers as soon they start to fade. In many instances this prolongs the availability of nectar for pollinators by encouraging more flowering sideshoots to develop. Annuals are best deadheaded by hand, by pinching out the faded bloom just below the flower. For perennials such as meadow phlox (*Phlox maniculata*) cutting back the central part of the old flowered stems with secateurs will encourage a second, smaller flush of flowers later in the season.

Although it is sensible to cut back plants promptly and dispose of diseased leaves and stems to prevent spores from overwintering in the soil, most herbaceous perennials can be left uncut until late winter or early spring. Postponing cutting them back will provide food for birds and a place for beneficial insects to hibernate over winter without disruption. The hollow stems of plants such as angelica and fennel (*Foeniculum vulgare*) are among the ladybug's favorite hibernation sites. You can encourage ladybugs to overwinter in your garden by cutting back plants with hollow stems in fall, and stacking the cut stems in a dry, sheltered corner where they will be undisturbed.

## Pruning shrubs and climbers to provide shelter and food

Experienced gardeners know that the timing of pruning is critical. If, for example, you prune evergreen shrubs too early in spring or late in summer, they produce lots of lush new growth that is likely to be damaged by frost or strong winds. The timing of pruning is even more crucial if you wish to support wildlife, because you want to minimize any disruption to creatures that rely on plants for shelter or food.

Mature ivy is a favorite nesting site for small birds. To minimize any disturbance to nesting birds and insects that feed and over-winter on the plant, pruning should be confined to late spring or early summer.

When you use the Directory always check whether the section on caring for plants gives an optimum time for pruning. Ivy (*Hedera*) is a vigorous evergreen vine that can be pruned any time of the year, but to reduce any disturbance to nesting birds, it's best undertaken in late spring or early summer. Another advantage of pruning ivy at this time of the year is that there is minimal disruption to the caterpillars of the Holly Blue butterfly, which feed and overwinter on the plant.

Although continually cutting hedges can deprive wildlife of a vital source of shelter and food, most hedges benefit from an annual trim. To avoid disturbing nesting birds and hibernating insects, evergreen plants should be left unpruned until mid or late summer. As a rule, delay pruning fruiting hedges until the birds have finished foraging for the berries.

Ideally, hedges should be pruned into an "A" shape, so that they have a slightly wider base. Not only does this look good and allow light to reach leaves at the base, but it also provides more protection for wildlife. If you live in an area with heavy snowfalls, a gently sloping top also minimizes snow from damaging it in winter. After pruning, always apply a balanced slow-release fertilizer around the base of the plant to replenish nutrients, and mulch with well-rotted manure or garden compost.

Several of the shrubs in the Directory, including firethorn (*Pyracantha*) and flowering quince (*Chaenomeles*), are ideal for training against a fence or wall. Once a permanent framework of branches has been established, a wall-trained firethorn will need pruning twice a year. In spring any outward-growing shoots should be cut back and other shoots shortened, so that the plant does not overrun its allotted space. In late summer, to reveal the ripening berries, shorten to two or three leaves any new shoots that are not to be used for tying in. After pruning, tie in the new growth using soft garden twine, and replace any ties that have broken or become too tight.

## Pruning a wall-trained firethorn

1 Wearing stout gardening gloves and goggles as protection against the sharp thorns, shorten to two or three leaves, any new shoots that are not to be used for tying in. This reveals the developing berries.

2 Remove any weak, dead or damaged growth completely, cutting back to the point of origin.

3 Using soft garden twine, securely tie in the new growth to a network of galvanized wires. This is a good time to check for ties that are broken or over-tight, which risk damaging the stems.

## Dividing a marsh marigold (*Caltha palustris*)

1 Pull apart the plant and divide into sections using a sharp knife. Make sure that each has a strong root system and several healthy shoots.

2 Trim back long roots and top growth with secateurs by between one third and one half.

3 Replant younger divisions of the plant around the edges of the pond in a burlap-lined container filled with aquatic compost.

4 Leave plant material that is not to be reused next to the edges of the pond for several days before composting. This allows any creatures that have been displaced to re-enter the water.

### Caring for water plants

A carefully planted wildlife pond will require minimal maintenance. The ideal time to do this is in late summer or early autumn, when there will be least disruption to wildlife. Avoid disturbing wildlife ponds in spring, when amphibians are breeding, or when the weather is very cold and they are hibernating. Using an aquarium net, remove unwanted pondweeds and any leaves or debris that have blown into the water. Large clumps of marginal perennials such as marsh marigold (*Caltha palustris*) can be divided, and the younger portions replanted around the edges of the pond. Unused plant material should be left at the edge of the water for several days, to allow any wildlife to re-enter the water safely. Small creatures can easily become entangled between the tough filaments of blanket weed. To make it easier for them to escape and return to the pond, try cutting the strands into smaller pieces before laying them out next to the pond.

Ponds need to be drained every few years to allow decaying material to be removed and any necessary repairs undertaken. To reduce the amount of disturbance to creatures that live in the pond try to plan this work so that it can be carried out in a single day.

## Dealing with pests and diseases

One of the best precautions you can take is to make sure that your plants are always adequately fed and watered. Healthy, strong specimens are much less likely to be targeted by pests and diseases than those that have been weakened by insufficient water or nutrients. Wherever possible select disease-resistant cultivars, and always choose plants that are right for your soil conditions and site.

Because of the risks to beneficial wildlife, take steps to reduce your use of chemicals, instead relying on a combination of natural predators, cultural methods and naturally occurring biological controls to deal with insect pests and diseases. Bear in mind that even those sprays that are marketed as "wildlife-friendly" are unselective in their effects and will affect the balance of beneficial insects in your garden. Products based on pyrethrum and derris, which are commonly recommended for controlling aphids, are harmful to ladybug larvae — one of the aphids' natural predators. Even if you follow the manufacturer's instructions and spray late in the day, you may harm beneficial insects that feed or shelter on flowers at night.

### Aphids

You can often eradicate small colonies of aphids by directing a strong jet of water at the affected part of the plant. Alternatively, rub them off with your fingers. Be patient and avoid spraying as soon as you see aphids. Natural predators like ladybugs will usually appear once there are sufficient numbers to sustain them. If the infestation is severe, try spot spraying colonies with soapy water. If you decide to do this, avoid spraying ladybugs or their larvae by moving them to another plant before targeting the area.

### Caterpillars

You can minimize the damage caused by moth and butterfly caterpillars by picking them off by hand as soon as you see them and replacing them on the leaves of another, less conspicuous plant. Putting up nesting boxes is a good idea, because some parent birds seek out caterpillars to feed their young. Pheromone traps are a simple yet effective method of controlling damage to fruit trees caused by codling moth caterpillars. A

biological control based on a naturally occurring bacterium, *Bacillus thuringiensis* (*Bt*) is sometimes recommended, for example, for heavy infestations of native trees. Sadly, *Bt* is indiscriminate in its effects and has been responsible for reducing the populations of many rare native North American butterflies and moths, including the lilac-winged Gaura moth.

### Powdery mildew

Some perennials such as phlox and monarda are susceptible to powdery mildew during prolonged dry spells. You can reduce the risk of this by selecting one of the mildew-resistant cultivars listed in the Directory and by making sure that the soil they are grown in does not dry out completely in summer. Following good gardening practices, such as increasing the circulation of air around plants and watering at ground level rather than from above, also helps.

### Slugs and snails

Because slugs and snails love young plants it is essential to protect tender, young seedlings until they are established. A popular method is to create a barrier around vulnerable plants, which the mollusks are unwilling to cross. Crushed eggshells, cut hair, sharp grit, and oatmeal are some of the diverse household materials that have proved to be effective in halting slugs and snails in their tracks. Soil-dwelling slugs can be dealt with through the use of a biological control based on a microscopic nematode, *Phasmarhabditis hermaphrodita*, which is watered into warm, damp soil. Beer traps are another safe way to deal with them, and can be easily put together at home. Encouraging frogs to take up residence in your garden will also help, because they feed on slugs.

### Whitefly

Yellow sticky flypapers are useful for catching greenhouse pests like whitefly and a good indication of when to introduce the biological control *Encarsia formosa*. For best results put the papers up just above the plants, rather than the top of the greenhouse where they may trap bees and flower flies. Whenever you go past gently brush the plants so that any flying insects are disturbed, fly up and get stuck on the traps.

# PLANT DIRECTORY

# Using the symbols in this book

These symbols appear below the name of each plant so you can quickly choose a suitable plant at a glance. They indicate which adverse geographical and climactic conditions a plant will thrive in and which animal or insect is especially encouraged by its presence in the garden.

## Height

 This symbol indicates how tall the plant will grow after 10 years. Perennials attain this size after their first year or two.

## Spread

 This symbol indicates how wide the plant will grow after 10 years. Perennials attain this size after their first year or two.

## When in Flower

These symbols give a general indication of when the plant is in flower.

   Spring

   Summer

   Autumn

   Winter

## Best Growing Position

Plants have varying requirements for sunlight: some will thrive in a wide range of growing positions, while others have precise needs for sun or shade.

   Full sun

   Partial shade

   Full shade

   Sun or shade

   Sun or partial shade

   Partial or full shade

## Wildlife

These symbols indicate the insects, birds, amphibians or mammals that are particularly attracted to the plant.

   Amphibian

   Bee

   Butterfly

   Caterpillar

   Bird

   Ladybug

   Flower fly

   Lacewing

## Zone Chart

Zones designate the lowest range of temperatures in which a plant will normally survive. Thus a plant in Zone 8 will normally survive between 10°F and 20°F (-12°C and -6°C).

| ZONE | °FAHRENHEIT | °CELSIUS |
|------|-------------|----------|
| 1 | Below -50 | Below -45 |
| 2 | -50 to -40 | -45 to -40 |
| 3 | -40 to -30 | -40 to -34 |
| 4 | -30 to -20 | -34 to -29 |
| 5 | -20 to -10 | -29 to -23 |
| 6 | -10 to 0 | -23 to -18 |
| 7 | 0 to 10 | -18 to -12 |
| 8 | 10 to 20 | -12 to -6 |
| 9 | 20 to 30 | -6 to -1 |
| 10 | 30 to 40 | -1 to 5 |
| 11 | above 40 | above 5 |

# *Achillea* cultivars
## Yarrow

### Zones 3–9

Achillea cultivars are drought-tolerant, hardy perennials that flower over a long period in summer and early autumn. The flat, platelike flowerheads, held on upright stems, provide a stable landing platform for beneficial insects, such as flower flies and ladybugs, which help to keep colonies of aphids at bay. The cultivars are generally less vigorous than the species, including the mat-forming and invasive *A. millefolium*, which is the bane of any well-maintained lawn.

Tall forms suitable for the back of a sunny border include *A. filipendulina* 'Cloth of Gold', with deep golden-yellow flowers, and the mustard-yellow *A.* 'Coronation Gold'. Midborder options include *A.* 'Moonshine', which has sulfur-yellow flowers, and *A. millefolium* 'Paprika', which has orange-red flowerheads fading to burnished gold, and often bears flowers of both colors at the same time, creating an attractive bicolored effect.

*If you have sensitive skin always wear gloves when working with achillea. Contact with the feathery, light green or gray-green foliage may aggravate skin.*

### Where to plant

Grow achillea in moist but well-drained soil that is not too rich. The choice of site is important because achillea cultivars can be killed by waterlogged soils. Plant in small groups toward the middle or back of a sunny mixed or herbaceous border, together with late-blooming perennials that have spiky or spire-like flowers, such as salvia and eryngium.

### Caring for plants

Do not use nitrogen-rich fertilizers. Before the flowers appear, loosely support medium and tall plants with brushwood or a "cat's cradle" constructed out of bamboo canes and garden twine. To provide shelter for overwintering insects, do not cut back until early spring, when large clumps can also be divided for use in other parts of the garden.

*Achillea* 'Walther Funcke' is considered to be one of the best red cultivars because its flowers retain their color well.

## Agastache foeniculum

### Anise hyssop

#### Zones 5–9

Anise hyssop is a versatile and long-flowering North American perennial, loved equally by insects and birds. If seed is sown indoors in early spring, by midsummer plants will have produced leafy, upright spires topped with dense clusters of tiny, violet-blue flowers. These are a long-lasting, nectar-rich treat for bees and

*Agastache urticifolia* 'Licorice White' is a fast-growing cultivar that flowers only 10 weeks after sowing.

some of the most commonly found butterflies, including the Red Admiral and Painted Lady. Small, seed-eating birds, such as goldfinches, find the decorative seedheads irresistible, and they hold up well into the winter months. The aniseed-scented leaves that give the plant its common name may be harvested while still young, and used for flavoring food or making herbal tea.

The powder-blue *A.* 'Blue Fortune' is one of the best cultivars for attracting butterflies and bees. *A. foeniculum* 'Alabaster' produces tidy clumps of creamy white flowers. Both are considerably shorter than the violet-blue species, making them excellent midborder companions for plants with gray or silver foliage. In warm zones, hummingbirds find the vibrant red-purple flowers of giant hummingbird mint (*A. barberi*) particularly alluring.

#### Where to plant

Anise hyssop prefers the same type of conditions as lavender: fertile, well-drained soil in full sun. Strongly upright in habit, it is perfect for adding vertical interest toward the back or middle of a sheltered, sunny border and is particularly suitable for planting in confined spaces. To attract a wide range of beneficial insects, combine it with small clumps of achillea, anthemis and monarda.

#### Caring for plants

In hot, dry summers anise hyssop may be affected by powdery mildew. To minimize the risk of this taking hold apply a deep, moisture-retaining mulch around the base of the plants and water well during dry spells. To provide food for small, seed-eating birds delay cutting back the faded flowerheads until spring, when large clumps can be divided.

Facing page: Anise hyssop is one of the most popular plants for butterfly and bee gardens.

# *Ajuga reptans* and cultivars

## Bugleweed, bugle

### Zones 3–9

Bugleweed is a dependable, evergreen, groundcover plant, perfect for colonizing areas of bare earth at the front of the border. It quickly spreads to form a lustrous, weed-suppressing carpet of spoon-shaped, deep green leaves. The small, leafy spires of dark blue flowers that emerge from the foliage in late spring to early summer are a valuable source of nectar for bees, especially bumblebees, which require continuous summer blooms. Butterflies, flower flies and ladybugs visit large swaths of flowering bugleweed. Although it is useful in wildflower gardens, take care about the position of the wild species, which is potentially invasive and may overwhelm smaller, less vigorous plants. Cultivated varieties are generally better behaved and include forms with pink flowers and multicolored or variegated leaves.

   *A. reptans* 'Burgundy Glow', which has dark blue flowers and cream-edged, magenta-tinted, silvery-green leaves, is one of the most attractive multicolored forms, providing a colorful, low carpet. 'Catlin's Giant', which bears spires, 8 in. (20 cm) tall, of deep blue flowers and large,

bronze-purple leaves, is a particularly vigorous variety and perfect for covering large areas of ground.

### Where to plant

Bugleweed grows well in any moist, well-drained soil in sun or partial shade. Plant 10 to 12 in. (25 to 30 cm) apart in groups toward the front of the border. It is a valuable plant for awkward, shady areas where grass will not grow, although some of the eye-catching foliage forms need sun to thrive.

### Caring for plants

To minimize the risk of powdery mildew, water well during dry spells. Rejuvenate by lifting and dividing congested clumps in early spring every second year, applying a mulch of well-rotted garden compost or leaf mold around the base of the new plants.

The blue-lipped flowers of *Ajuga* reptans are specially adapted for cross-fertilization by bees.

# Amelanchier species

## Juneberry, shadbush, snowy mespilus

### Zones 4–9

Amelanchiers are deciduous, multistemmed large shrubs or small trees, grown for their striking autumn color and summer fruits. The oblong to elliptic leaves are often tinged with bronze when they emerge, maturing to mid- or dark green before turning bonfire shades of vermilion and orange in fall. In early and midspring the branches are smothered with masses of star-shaped white flowers — an important source of nectar for butterflies and solitary, early-season bees. The purple-black fruit that follows the flowers may be eaten cooked, but wildlife-friendly gardeners will leave them on the tree where they will quickly be devoured by songbirds and small mammals, such as squirrels and foxes.

The suckering shadbush (*A. canadensis*) supports at least a dozen types of birds, from diminutive robins and larks through to larger jays and woodpeckers. It is particularly suitable for small gardens. Downy serviceberry (*A. arborea*) is a small tree native to North America that reaches a height of 25 ft. (8 m) and a spread of 20 ft. (6 m) in maturity. Snowy mespilus (*A. lamarckii*) is an elegant, upright shrub or small tree. One of the larger species, snowy mespilus can be successfully coppiced and under-planted with a carpet of woodland-edge plants.

### Where to plant

Amelanchiers prefer fertile, moist but well-drained, neutral to acidic soil — they are not suitable for sites with chalky, alkaline soil. Acidic soils produce superior autumn color. Specimens look best when they are set against a dark or evergreen background in a partially shady area of a shrub border or woodland edge.

### Caring for plants

Cut stems growing too close together to ground level each winter. Also, check the spread of *A. canadensis* by removing rooted suckers at ground level in winter. *A. lamarckii* may be coppiced every three years by cutting all the branches down to ground level. After pruning, apply a generous mulch of composted pine needles or well-rotted leaf mold around the base of the plant.

Juneberry flowers are an important source of nectar for butterflies and solitary, early-season bees.

# *Anethum graveolens* and cultivars

## Dill, dill weed

### Zones 3–11

Dill is one of the best hardy annual herbs for encouraging a wide range of beneficial insects to take up residence in the garden. Easily grown from seed, it bears flat, umbrella-like heads of tiny, yellow flowers on stiff, hollow stems in midsummer, and these make perfectly designed landing platforms for insects. An invaluable food source for caterpillars of the Black Swallowtail butterfly, the feathery, blue-green foliage provides a delicate foil against which the flowers of herbaceous perennials can be seen. If they are harvested while still young, the leaves add a subtle aniseed-like flavor to fish dishes, salads and sauces.

Bolt-resistant cultivars include *A. g.* 'Dukat', which has abundant, highly aromatic foliage, and the compact 'Fern Leaved', which is particularly suitable for growing in pots.

### Where to plant

Grow in fertile, well-drained, neutral to slightly acidic soil. Plant in small groups in a sunny area of the herb garden, toward the front of the flower border or in a large terracotta pot. Because dill self-seeds freely, take care to choose a spot where you would like it to appear year after year. Avoid planting near fennel because the two herbs may cross-pollinate, and dill's distinctive flavor may be lost.

### Caring for plants

During prolonged dry spells dill quickly runs to seed. Avoid this by choosing bolt-resistant cultivars and water well during the growing season. To harvest the seeds, remove the seedheads two to three weeks after the plant has finished flowering, when the seeds are beginning to turn brown. Dry in a brown paper bag until the seeds come away easily, and store them in an airtight jar.

The tiny yellow flowers of dill have short nectar tubes, which are ideal for flower flies to feed from.

# Angelica gigas

## Korean angelica

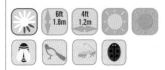

6ft
1.8m

4ft
1.2m

### Zones 4–9

Korean angelica is a statuesque, summer-flowering biennial, loved by many of the beneficial bugs that help to control insect pests. In the first year it sends up an impressive display of coarsely toothed, midgreen leaves, similar to those of bugbane (*Actaea*). The following year tall, maroon-tinted stems arise from the foliage, topped with dome-shaped heads of rich purple flowers. From midsummer these are literally buzzing with beneficial parasitic wasps, ladybugs and lacewings.

One of the drawbacks of Korean angelica is that it dies after flowering. Given the right conditions, it will self-seed, although the intensity of color in the seedlings may vary. Many gardeners claim that a dark maroon-flowered form of wild angelica, *A. sylvestris* 'Vicar's Mead', is a more reliable plant. *A. gigas* 'Gold Leaf' is a new form available from specialist nurseries; it has burnished golden-yellow foliage and beet-red flowers and stems.

### Where to plant

Grow in moist, fertile soil in sun or partial shade. Use singly or in groups to make a dramatic statement, placing plants toward the back of the herbaceous or mixed border, along a woodland edge or in the moist margins of a pond or stream.

### Caring for plants

Use beer traps or eco-friendly pellets to protect the tender, young foliage from slugs and snails. Water well, especially during long, hot spells. To guarantee a supply of food for small birds and fresh plants for next year, do not remove the faded flowerheads until the following spring. In spring transplant small, emerging seedlings to their final flowering positions.

Beneficial insects, including ladybugs, are attracted to Korean angelica, which bears masses of small flowers with easy access to nectar.

# Anthemis tinctoria

## Golden marguerite, ox-eye chamomile

### Zones 3–7

Golden marguerites are one of the best summer-flowering perennials for encouraging a wide range of beneficial insects. Produced over many weeks on slender, upright stems, the daisy-like flowers are highly attractive to no fewer than five types of beneficial bugs (flower flies, lacewings, ladybugs, tachinid flies and parasitic mini-wasps). Although this is a short-lived plant, its longevity can be improved by cutting the faded flower stems and ferny, aromatic foliage back hard to the ground immediately after flowering. The plant will regenerate from the base and may even produce a second, smaller flush of flowers in autumn.

A. t. 'Kelwayi' forms a low mound of clear golden-yellow flowers and deeply divided, midgreen leaves; A. t. 'E.C. Buxton' has pale lemon-yellow flowers with contrasting, darker yellow centers.

Facing page: *Anthemis punctata* subsp. *cupaniana* forms low mounds of long-lasting, white daisy-like flowers.

### Where to plant

Golden marguerites are a good choice for a sunny site with poor but well-drained soil. For maximum impact, plant in bold swaths, together with late-bloomers, such as black-eyed Susan (*Rudbeckia*) and sneezeweed (*Helenium*), which will extend the season of interest beyond late summer and often until the first frosts.

### Caring for plants

In spring, use beer traps or eco-friendly pellets to protect plants from slug and snail damage. Well before the flowers appear, erect brushwood supports or link stakes to support the stems. To provide autumn food for small birds, wait for several weeks until after plants have finished flowering before cutting back the faded stems.

Golden marguerites will thrive in a sunny spot with well-drained chalky soil.

# *Antirrhinum majus*

## Snapdragon

### Zones 4–11

Snapdragons are colorful tender perennials, usually grown as annuals, which are loved by bees, butterflies and birds. Easily grown from seed sown indoors and planted out after all risk of frost has passed, they produce upright stems of fragrant, tubular, two-lipped flowers and lance-shaped, green or bronze-purple leaves. On warm days from midsummer onward

Snapdragons are one of the favorite host plants of the Common Buckeye and Checkerspot butterflies.

bumblebees in search of nectar land on the lower lips of the flowers. Even after they have finished flowering snapdragons continue to play an important wildlife role because they produce copious quantities of seed, which provides food for many small songbirds and also, in the right conditions, an opportunity for the plant to self-seed.

Snapdragons are available as single- and bicolored blooms, in almost every color and shade — except blue. *A. m.* 'Black Prince', which produces sumptuous, dark crimson flowers on wine-red stems 18 in. (45 cm) tall, is one of the older midborder varieties that is particularly attractive to wildlife. The plants in the *A. m.* Rocket Series have tall, single-colored spikes to 36 in. (90 cm) high, in shades of pink, red, yellow, bronze and white. A reliable, repeat-flowering form, it is valuable for use in cut-flower arrangements. The dwarf, early-flowering *A. m.* Floral Showers Series produces single bicolored blooms on stems to 8 in. (20 cm) high.

### Where to plant

Snapdragons need fertile, well-drained soil and a sunny site. For maximum impact, plant in generous drifts toward the back, middle or front of the border. Dwarf forms can be grown in pots, while trailing forms are ideal for a hanging basket or wall-mounted container.

### Caring for plants

Transplanted seedlings must be watered regularly for several weeks until they are well established. Support tall cultivars with a framework of small, twiggy branches. Pick off caterpillars feeding at the front of the border and replace them on the leaves of plants in less prominent positions. To prolong flowering, remove spent flowers regularly and apply a liquid fertilizer each month. To provide food for birds, do not cut back the plants immediately after they have finished flowering.

# *Aquilegia* species and cultivars
## Columbine

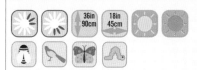

### Zones 3–8

Columbines have distinctive floral spurs that play a vital role in luring insect and bird pollinators. The nodding heads of tubular flowers, borne on slender, upright stems above mounds of fern-like, dark or midgreen leaves, are popular features of late spring and early summer gardens. The unique architecture of the flowers encourages visits from long-tongued nectar-feeders, such as bumblebees, butterflies and Hawk moths. After flowering, the dried seedpods split to reveal numerous tiny, black seeds that guarantee columbine a place in the border year after year.

Growers and seed merchants offer a wide range of flowers in both bright colors and pastel shades. To encourage wildlife, choose a species or one of the long-spurred hybrids such as *A.* McKana Group, which produces single- and bicolored flowers in shades of blue, yellow and rose-red, or *A.* 'Crimson Star', with clusters of two or three carmine-red and creamy white flowers on each stem. In warm zones hummingbirds are attracted to the bright coral-red and yellow blooms of *A. canadensis* (eastern wild columbine) and *A. formosa* (western columbine).

*Take care when handling the plants because contact with the sap may cause skin irritation.*

### Where to plant

Columbines hate poor drainage so choose a spot with fertile, moisture-retentive but well-drained soil in direct sun or dappled shade. Because the foliage can start to look untidy after flowering, columbines are best grown behind late-blooming perennials, which can take over when the plants die back.

### Caring for plants

Plants affected by powdery mildew should be cut back to ground level; then water and feed them. To provide a treat for small birds and a chance for the plant to self-seed, leave the faded flowerheads in place for as long as possible. In early spring remove any unwanted self-sown seedlings and mulch the remaining plants with a generous layer of well-rotted compost or manure.

Columbine seeds are a particular favorite of sparrows and finches.

# *Aruncus dioicus*

## Goatsbeard, bride's feathers

### Zones 3–8

Goatsbeard plays an important role in supporting the young population of the Dusky Azure butterfly. The caterpillars feed on the fern-like midgreen leaflets in spring, and the foliage provides shelter for hibernating chrysalises. For a few weeks in early or midsummer, the creamy white or greenish white plumes of frothy flowers, held on tall, upright stems, will be buzzing with bees. One of the drawbacks of this imposing perennial is its size — many gardens simply may not have the space that it requires to shine.

The cultivated form *A. d.* 'Kneiffii' is more compact than the species and is therefore suitable for average gardens.

### Where to plant

Grow goatsbeard in moist, fertile soil that has previously been enriched with well-rotted organic matter. A versatile, wildlife-friendly specimen plant for the back of a large border, a water garden or woodland edge, it is best grown in a sunny spot that remains reliably moist over the summer months. When it grows in partial or deep shade the plant produces fewer blooms. Nectar-rich plants, such as wood geranium (*Geranium maculatum*), that are loved by adult butterflies make excellent companions.

### Caring for plants

Water well during prolonged hot, dry spells. To provide shelter for overwintering insects do not cut back the faded stems until late winter or early spring. Afterward, apply a generous mulch of well-rotted garden compost or manure around the base of the plant.

The fluffy, greenish white blooms of goatsbeard look wonderful set against a green backdrop.

# Asclepias tuberosa

## Butterfly weed, silkweed

### Zones 3–10

Butterfly weed is a drought-tolerant perennial loved by butterflies, bumblebees and hummingbirds. The plant plays an important role in each part of the lifecycle of the Monarch butterfly. In late spring whorls of slender, light to midgreen leaves provide sustenance for the emerging caterpillars, and from midsummer to early autumn the adults feed on the showy, orange-red, nectar-rich flowers. This diet provides a chemical defense that makes the butterflies unpalatable to birds at each stage of their development. In fall decorative, spindle-shaped seedpods develop. These split to reveal numerous seeds with silky tails, which allow the seeds to be distributed long distances in the wind.

*Take care when handling the plants — contact with the sap may cause skin irritation.*

### Where to plant

Butterfly weed prefers a sunny spot with well-drained, loamy soil. Encourage butterflies by planting in generous groups with other nectar-rich plants, such as purple coneflower (*Echinacea purpurea*), black-eyed Susan (*Rudbeckia*) and lantana.

### Caring for plants

To prolong flowering, deadhead regularly during the summer months. Try not to move established specimens because the deep taproot does not transplant well. To allow overwintering insects a place to shelter, do not remove the silky seedheads and faded foliage until the following spring.

The showy flowers of butterfly weed are arranged in umbrella-like clusters, providing a stable landing pad for insect diners.

## *Aster* cultivars

### New England aster, Michaelmas daisy

### Zones 3–8

Asters are one of the star perennials of the late-summer border. From late summer on they produce sprays of long-lasting, blue, pink, lavender-blue or occasionally white daisy-like flowers on stout, upright stems above clumps of dark green pointed leaves. The flowers are an important source of nectar for butterflies and bees preparing for winter hibernation, and the ripening seedheads provide valuable autumn food for small birds.

*A.* x *frikartii* 'Mönch', with yellow-centered, lavender-blue flowers, is unmistakably the best midborder aster because it is particularly long-flowering, is unaffected by mildew and seldom needs staking. The blue-flowered *A.* x *f.* 'Wunder von Stäfa' is similar in size. *A. novae-angliae* 'Andenken an Alma Pötschke', a tall cultivar with glowing, bright salmon-pink flowers, is perfect for the back of the border.

### Where to plant

Grow in moist but well-drained, moderately fertile soil. Depending on the type, plant singly or in small groups, toward either the middle or back of the border. Asters work particularly well with other late-summer perennials, such as yarrow (*Achillea*), solidago and veronicastrum.

### Caring for plants

To stave off powdery mildew, water regularly during dry spells. Stake tall varieties with bamboo canes or brushwood in early spring. Encourage midborder varieties to be self-supporting by pinching out the growing tips in early summer. To provide food for birds leave the faded flowerheads in place until the following spring.

The bright rose-pink flowers of *Aster novae-angliae* 'Barr's Pink' provide a late-season feast for butterflies and bees.

# *Aurinia saxatilis* (syn. *Alyssum saxatile*)

## Gold dust

### Zones 3–8

Gold dust is a sturdy, ground-hugging perennial, ideal for carpeting sunny areas of a raised bed, rock garden or bank. It is one of the easiest alpines to grow from seed, quickly forming low mounds of hairy, gray-green leaves. The evergreen foliage makes gold dust particularly useful for softening the edges of hard landscaping. In late spring and early summer many beneficial insects, including bees, flower flies and ladybugs, visit the sprays of tiny, bright yellow flowers that smother the plant.

A. s. 'Citrina' bears flowers in a more intense shade of lemon-yellow than the species. The dwarf form A. s. 'Compacta', which grows to 4 in. (10 cm) high, works well where space is limited.

### Where to plant

Gold dust prefers a sunny spot with poor, well-drained soil. Planted in groups, it makes a robust wildlife-friendly edge for paths and borders — but avoid planting next to smaller, less vigorous plants, which could be overwhelmed by its spreading habit.

### Caring for plants

If specimens become infested with colonies of aphids in spring, spray with a mixture of water and liquid soap, or direct a strong jet of water at the insects to dislodge them. To maintain a compact, neat mound, cut back the woody stems lightly after the plant has flowered. Try to retain as many of the tiny seedheads as possible to provide food for small birds, and also an opportunity for the plant to self-seed.

Gold dust's tiny yellow flowers are attractive to several of the bugs that help the organic gardener keep colonies of insect pests at bay.

# Baptisia australis

## False indigo, wild blue indigo

### Zones 3–9

False indigo is a tall, drought-resistant perennial, ideal for areas that are difficult to get to for regular maintenance. Initially slow to become established, it produces vertical spikes of dark indigo-blue flowers from early to midsummer, which emerge from clumps of mid- to dark green leaflets. Bumblebees find these lupine-like blooms particularly alluring. False indigo is also an important host plant of the Wild Indigo Duskywing butterfly. The young caterpillars feed on the foliage, which contains a mild toxin that makes them unpalatable to predators. Unlike many other perennials, the plant continues to look good long after flowering. Its slender, branched stems and the inflated seedpods that develop in fall look beautiful frosted in the winter garden.

### Where to plant

False indigo thrives in well-drained, lime-free, sandy soil in full sun. Plant singly or in groups of three, allowing at least 36 in. (90 cm) between plants, and site them carefully because the plant is difficult to move once it has developed its deep taproot.

### Caring for plants

Water regularly until the plant is fully established. To provide food for seed-eating birds and shelter for overwintering insects, avoid cutting back until early spring.

In false indigo's native prairie setting its vertical spikes act as a signpost, ensuring that it is easily seen by insect pollinators.

# *Berberis* cultivars

## Japanese barberry

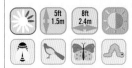

### Zones 4–8

Planting one of the showy garden hybrids of Japanese barberry is an eye-catching way of providing wildlife with shelter and food. Small birds often build nests among the spiny branches, where they are safe from predators, and in spring the clusters of inconspicuous, pale yellow flowers provide nectar for butterflies and bees. But it is in fall when this deciduous shrub really shines. The foliage turns spectacular shades of orange and red — a signal to the songbirds that devour the glossy, bright red berries that they are ripe and ready to eat.

Cultivated varieties of Japanese barberry offer numerous different shapes and colored foliage. They have been developed to be slower growing than the highly invasive *B. thunbergii* that has colonized large areas of North America. *B. t.* 'Aurea', which has bright golden-yellow spring foliage that turns orange-red in fall, is best reserved for areas of partial shade, because the delicate foliage can scorch in the midday sun. It is wonderful for illuminating dark green areas of a shrub, hedge or mixed border. The versatile *B. t.* f. *atropurpurea* makes a great specimen plant or informal hedge, the dark purple leaves turning glowing red in fall. *B. t.* f. *atropurpurea* 'Rose Glow' is a variegated form with pink-mottled, red-purple leaves, which turn orange and red in fall. Don't worry if you are sold a young specimen with resolutely purple leaves — the variegation starts to develop only during the second season.

*All parts of berberis may cause a mild stomach upset if eaten.*

### Where to plant

Hybrids of Japanese barberry are easily grown in any well-drained soil, and they can be planted in full sun or partial shade; they work equally well as single specimen plants or massed to form an informal fruiting hedge.

### Caring for plants

Japanese barberry requires minimal pruning. To minimize the loss of fall berries, delay cutting the plant back until mid- or late winter. Remove any dead or diseased shoots in midsummer, as they are clearly visible. After pruning, mulch around the base with well-rotted compost or manure.

The red-tinged yellow spring flowers of *Berberis* x *ottawensis* 'Superba' are a valuable source of nectar.

## *Buddleja davidii*
## Buddleia, butterfly bush

### Zones 5–10

Buddleias are indisputably the most important summer-flowering shrubs for attracting butterflies. If they are pruned hard annually in spring, plants remain compact enough for the smallest garden, producing a mass of honey-scented flower spikes on arching stems over a long period from midsummer. In fall the pointed, gray-green leaves gradually turn butter-yellow while the seedheads provide food for birds.

   *B. d.* 'Purple Emperor' is a new, compact form that is particularly suitable for smaller gardens; *B. d.* 'White Profusion', an elegant alternative to the ubiquitous purple forms, produces spectacular flower spikes often to 16 in. (40 cm) long.

### Where to plant

Grow in fertile, well-drained soil. Plant singly or, if there is space, in small groups toward the back of a sunny mixed or shrub border with other butterfly-friendly shrubs and perennials, such as lavender, hebe, stonecrop and scabious.

### Caring for plants

Buddleias are trouble-free plants. To provide food for small birds and shelter for overwintering insects, do not cut back the faded flower spikes until early spring. Then, prune hard, removing all the previous year's growth down to the last three or four buds, and mulch with well-rotted garden compost or manure.

Facing page: The lovely white-flowered *Buddleja davidii* 'White Profusion' is one of the forms of butterfly bush that is covered in butterflies in summer.

*Buddleja davidii* 'Black Knight' has striking dark purple flowers.

# Calendula officinalis

## Pot marigold

### Zones 6–10

Old-fashioned, aromatic pot marigolds are indispensable for attracting a wide range of beneficial pollinating insects to the garden in summer. One of the easiest annuals to grow from seed, they produce a succession of bright orange or yellow daisy-like flowers on upright stems almost continuously from early summer to midautumn. Left in place, the ripening seedheads will provide food for small birds and ensure that there are plenty of plants in the border the following year.

### Where to plant

Grow in well-drained, poor to moderately fertile soil. Plant in small groups toward the front of a sunny mixed or cottage-style border, or use for brightening areas of the herb or vegetable garden.

### Caring for plants

Deadhead regularly in summer and early fall to prolong flowering. After this, leave seedheads to ripen to provide food for small birds. Remove faded foliage and any unwanted self-sown seedlings in spring.

In addition to brightening rows of vegetables, pot marigolds help to suppress weeds and keep aphids at bay.

# *Caltha palustris*
## Marsh marigold, kingcup

### Zones 3–9

Marsh marigolds are valuable aquatic perennials for a bog garden or the moist margins of a small wildlife pond. They are one of the first water plants to bloom, producing a mass of waxy, yellow, buttercup-like flowers on hollow, branching stems from early spring. The flowers are a welcome early source of nectar for butterflies and bees, and the lustrous, kidney-shaped leaves that often appear later than the flowers provide shelter for small insects such as beetles.

The more compact *C. p.* var. *alba* has yellow-centered, white flowers.

### Where to plant

Grow marsh marigolds in the rich, fertile soil of a bog garden or around the margins of a pond, in water that is no more than 9 in. (23 cm) deep.

To attract butterflies, plant in small groups rather than singly. Watermint (*Mentha spicata*) and the curious corkscrew rush (*Juncus effusus* f. *spiralis*) make excellent companions.

### Caring for plants

To prevent mildew taking hold in summer, make sure that the soil is always moist. Lift and divide large clumps in late summer, replanting the younger portions around the edges of the pond. Leave the older parts of the plant that are not to be replanted next to the pond for several days, so that any small creatures sheltering in the foliage can escape back into the water.

The bright yellow flowers of marsh marigold often appear before the kidney-shaped leaves unfurl.

# *Caryopteris* x *clandonensis* cultivars

## Bluebeard, blue spiraea

### Zones 5–9

Bluebeard, a small, woody shrub, which is usually treated as a perennial, is a late-season magnet for butterflies and bees. From late summer clusters of cobalt or lavender-blue flowers are borne on upright stems of slender, aromatic, gray-green leaves. The blooms are a useful source of nectar when many other summer shrubs and perennials have finished flowering, and if they are left intact the ripening seedheads provide food for small birds.

Among the best cultivars are *C.* x *c.* 'Heavenly Blue', which has a particularly upright habit and piercing deep blue flowers; the dark blue-flowered *C.* x *c.* 'Kew Blue', which has gray-green leaves, silvery green beneath; and *C.* x *c.* 'Worcester Gold', with vibrant chartreuse-yellow foliage, which contrasts beautifully with the lavender-blue flowers.

### Where to plant

Grow in moderately fertile, light, well-drained soil. Plant singly toward the front of a sunny shrub or mixed border. Where winter temperatures fall below 5°F (-15°C), grow against a sheltered south- or west-facing wall.

### Caring for plants

Remove and destroy any leaves distorted by capsid bugs. To provide food for small birds avoid cutting back until the following year. In early spring prune all the flowered stems back hard to the last three or four buds, and mulch generously around the base of the plant. Established plants develop a woody framework, which should not be cut into.

Don't worry if some of the stems of bluebeard are killed by frost — the plant will produce new growth from the base in spring.

# *Ceanothus* evergreen cultivars

## California lilac, blue blossom

6ft 1.8m   6ft 1.8m

### Zones 4–8

Evergreen varieties of California lilac provide a useful nesting site for small and medium-sized songbirds. The branches of this bushy, spreading shrub are covered with glossy, finely toothed, dark or midgreen leaves, which provide both good cover against predators and food for the emerging caterpillars of many common butterflies and moths. In late spring and early summer the branches are smothered in fluffy clusters of rich blue flowers. The flowers are a good source of nectar for butterflies and bees. After it has finished flowering, California lilac is a home for the insects on which many songbirds feed.

There are several evergreen cultivars of California lilac, offering a range of different shapes and garden uses. The spreading *C.* 'Blue Cushion', which has dark blue flowers in late spring and early summer and grows to 6 ft. (1.8 m), can be trained as a wall shrub where space is limited. *C.* 'Blue Mound', with dark blue flowers in late spring, is a mound-forming cultivar growing 5 x 6 ft. (1.5 x 1.8 m), which is perfect for softening the edges of a low wall. The bushy *C.* 'Burkwoodii', which has bright blue flowers in late summer and early autumn, will eventually grow 5 x 6 ft. (1.5 x 1.8 m). Rarely exceeding 5 ft. (1.5 m), *C.* 'Southmead', which bears dark blue flowers in late spring and early summer, is particularly suitable for small gardens. *C. thyrsiflorus* 'Skylark' bears dark blue flowers in late spring and early summer and is a cultivated form of one of the hardiest species.

### Where to plant

California lilac grows best in a sunny, well-drained spot protected from cold, drying winds. Although tolerant of mildly alkaline soils, the leaves will show signs of interveinal chlorosis if it is grown on limestone or thin chalk. Although usually grown as a free-standing shrub, the plant can be fan-trained against a sunny wall.

### Caring for plants

Reduce the shoots of forms that bloom in late spring and early summer by one-third in midsummer. Late-blooming forms should be pruned in the same way but in late spring, to minimize any disruption to overwintering insects and nesting birds. After pruning, apply a layer of well-rotted organic matter around the base of the plant and feed with a balanced liquid fertilizer.

*Ceanothus* leaves provide sustenance for the caterpillars of many butterflies and moths, including the Pale Swallowtail and Spring Azure butterflies.

# Centranthus ruber

## Red valerian, Jupiter's beard

**Zones 5–8**

Red valerian is a long-flowering, drought-tolerant perennial that provides a rich source of nectar for bees, butterflies and moths. Over a long period, from early summer to the first frosts, clusters of tiny, honey-scented, dark rose-pink, red or white flowers are borne on tall, upright stems. Many of the most common butterfly species find these irresistible, and night-flying moths are lured by the flowers' fragrance. Although useful for naturalizing in difficult areas of the garden, red valerian's tendency to self-seed vigorously may become a problem, especially when it starts to grow up through concrete or to damage the walls on which it is growing. White-flowered forms of valerian — C. r. 'Albus' and 'Snowcloud' and C. 'White Cloud' — are particularly attractive to night-flying pollinators such as Hawk moths.

### Where to plant

Although red valerian will grow in most well-drained, neutral to alkaline garden soils in sun or partial shade, flowering is superior in poor, dry conditions. For best results, choose a site that reproduces the conditions under which the plant grows in the wild, such as the base of a wall or a stony bank. Encourage butterflies by planting red valerian in generous drifts in combination with later blooming perennials, which will offer an alternative source of nectar once the plant has gone to seed.

### Caring for plants

Deadhead regularly in summer to encourage a second flush of flowers. To provide food for small birds and shelter for overwintering insects, delay cutting the plant down to the ground until the following spring. Any unwanted self-sown seedlings can be removed at this time.

Red valerian attracts some of the most common butterfly species, including the Mourning Cloak, Painted Lady and Great Spangled Fritillary.

# Cercis canadensis

## Eastern redbud

### Zones 4–9

The eastern redbud is a small, multistemmed tree grown for its early spring blossoms and ornamental seedpods. In maturity this relatively short-lived tree forms a graceful, vase-like shape with an ancient, gnarled appearance that belies its true age. The purplish pink, pea-like flowers that appear before the leaves are an important source of nectar for many early-flying butterflies and bees, while the flattened, bean-like seedpods that follow persist well through winter, providing food for several species of songbirds. The distinctive, heart-shaped leaves are red-bronze when they emerge but turn dark green and finally a soft shade of yellow before they fall.

Several cultivated varieties are available, offering variegated or dark purple foliage and pure white or pink flowers, and many of these blend more easily into the landscape than the purplish pink flowers of the species. *C. c.* 'Royal White' is a hardy, white-flowered form particularly suitable for planting in northern gardens. *C. c.* 'Silver Cloud', which has silvery-white, variegated leaves and magenta-pink flowers, is ideal for illuminating areas of light dappled shade, while *C. c.* 'Forest Pansy', which has rose-purple flowers and dark reddish purple leaves that fade with age, is an excellent foil for plants with silver-gray foliage.

### Where to plant

The eastern redbud makes an ideal specimen tree for a small or medium-sized wildlife garden, where it should be planted in the center of a lawn or sited near a patio or deck. For best results plant young trees in spring or autumn in fertile, moist but well-drained soil in direct sunlight or dappled shade. Careful consideration should be given to the final position of the tree because older specimens resent being transplanted.

### Caring for plants

Remove dead, diseased or crossing stems in early summer. To encourage good leaf color, well-established specimens can be successfully coppiced in early spring. After pruning apply a generous mulch of well-rotted compost around the base of the plant.

The flowers of the eastern redbud provide nectar for several common species of butterfly, including the Tiger Swallowtail, Spring Azure and Juvenal's Duskywing.

# *Chaenomeles* cultivars

## Flowering quince, Japanese quince

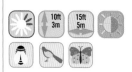

### Zones 5–9

Flowering quinces are hardy, deciduous shrubs, grown chiefly for their showy, apple-blossom-like spring flowers. Produced in clusters of two or four on bare, often spiny branches, the blooms are a vital source of nectar for early-flying butterflies and bees. The toothed leaves that follow the flowers emerge reddish bronze and mature to a lustrous, mid- or dark green before they are shed. In autumn small, aromatic, yellowish green, apple-like fruit develop, each 2 to 3 in. (5 to 8 cm) long. They can be harvested in midfall, cooked and made into preserve, but if they are left undisturbed the fallen fruits are popular with ground-feeding birds.

The most common flower color is bright red, but there are many cultivars with flowers in shades of pink and white. Although the spiny branches provide birds with some protection against predators, many gardeners prefer thornless varieties, which are both easier to handle and less likely to collect fallen leaves and other debris.

*C. speciosa* 'Contorta' is a new form with twisted stems and white flowers that is starting to appear in nurseries and garden centers. Its contorted branches make a wonderful ornamental feature in the winter garden. *C. speciosa* 'Nivalis', which has pure white flowers, is an especially vigorous upright form, eventually growing 8 x 15 ft. (2.4 x 5 m). *C. x superba* 'Jet Trail', a compact, white-flowering form with few thorns, grows 2 x 5 ft. (60 x 150 cm). *C. x superba* 'Texas Scarlet', which has bright red flowers, is a low-growing variety with almost thornless branches achieving a height and spread of about 40 in. (1 m). *C.* 'Toyo-Nishiki' often produces a combination of red, white and pink flowers all on the same branch. Growing 6 to 10 ft. (1.8 to 3 m) at maturity, it is useful for training against a sunny wall or in a mass planting.

### Where to plant

Although flowering quinces tolerate dry soil and partial shade, the best ornamental displays are achieved on plants growing in full sun. Depending on the variety, they may be planted as a single specimen or in groups to form an attractive boundary hedge.

### Caring for plants

Prune established specimens in late spring or early summer. Wear stout gardening gloves as protection against the thorns, remove any crossing branches and shorten all sideshoots to five or six leaves to maximize flowering the following spring.

Facing page: The open, cup-shaped flowers of *Chaenomeles speciosa* look wonderful frosted in the early spring garden.

## *Clematis tangutica* and cultivars

## Golden clematis, old man's beard

**Zones 4–9**

These late-flowering clematis are useful decorative plants in the garden, extending the season of interest to fall and beyond. Floriferous and easy to grow, they are hardy vines, producing masses of distinctive lantern- or bell-shaped, yellow or orange flowers from midsummer to midfall, often with contrasting brown or purplish centers. The flowers are a vital source of nectar for insects preparing for

Golden clematis seedheads become fluffier with time, providing food for small birds and interest in the winter garden.

hibernation, and the silvery seedheads that develop after the flowers fade are popular with birds in autumn and winter.

The group includes cultivars that are suitable for all sizes of garden. *C.* 'Bill MacKenzie', which has rich yellow, bell-shaped flowers and finely divided, midgreen leaves, is one of the best yellow-flowered forms. The species itself, *C. tangutica*, has small, canary-yellow, lantern-shaped flowers and is a vigorous plant, native to Tibet and northwest China; left unpruned, it can reach 20 x 10 ft. (6 x 3 m). In a small garden or on a patio, the less vigorous cultivar *C. t.* 'Radar Love' is similar but rarely exceeds 8 ft. (2.4 m). The new cultivar *C.* 'Last Dance', which grows 12 to 15 ft. (4 to 5 m) high, has small, orange-yellow, nodding flowers with contrasting reddish stems; it peaks in midfall, providing a wonderful source of food for late-flying butterflies and bees.

### Where to plant

Golden clematis thrive in most garden soils and will tolerate comparatively poor, dry conditions. Flowering best in a sunny position, they are ideal for growing over a wall, pergola or arch, or through a tall shrub or small tree. To encourage new shoots, plant clematis with the bottom 2 to 4 in. (5 to 10 cm) of the stems below ground level in a generous planting hole, adding several handfuls of bonemeal and good quality compost.

### Caring for plants

Golden clematis offer excellent resistance to clematis wilt, the debilitating fungal disease that sometimes affects large-flowered hybrid clematis. In early spring cut all stems back to just above an old leaf joint about 12 in. (30 cm) above ground level. This will produce a plant that is green from top to bottom and flowers at a level where they can easily be seen.

Facing page: Golden clematis have fleshy, four-petalled flowers in various shades of yellow.

# Coreopsis lanceolata

## Lanceleaf coreopsis, tickseed

### Zones 4–9

Lanceleaf coreopsis is one of the best perennials for supporting a wide range of butterflies and beneficial pollinating insects. As long as it is deadheaded regularly, it produces a succession of cheerful, chrome-yellow, daisy-like flowers over a long period from late spring to midsummer, which are held on slender, upright stems above weed-suppressing carpets of midgreen leaves. Even after flowering it continues to have an important wildlife use: the ripening seedheads are a favorite food of finches and other small, seed-eating birds.

### Where to plant

Grow in fertile, well-drained soil. Plant in bold drifts toward the middle of a sunny herbaceous border with late-blooming perennials, such as black-eyed Susan (*Rudbeckia*), gayfeather (*Liatris*) and solidago, which provide food for butterflies and other beneficial insects after the tickseed has gone over.

### Caring for plants

To encourage flowering, deadhead regularly and water well during hot, dry spells. Leave the faded flowerheads on the plant until the following spring to provide winter food for birds. Remove any unwanted self-sown seedlings in spring as part of routine border maintenance.

Birds are particularly attracted to the seeds of lanceleaf coreopsis.

## Coriandrum sativum
## Coriander

**Zones 3–11**

Coriander is one of the best annual herbs for helping to keep colonies of insect pests at bay without using chemical sprays. From midsummer to fall, flower flies, lacewings and ladybugs — three of the most efficient aphid-eaters in the organic gardener's arsenal — are lured by small, umbrella-shaped clusters of white or pale purple flowers on leafy stalks. Easily grown from seed sown in the garden in spring, it's also a useful companion plant — the pungent, bright green foliage helps deter carrot-fly. In fall coriander sets seed, which can be harvested as soon as it begins to turn golden-brown and then dried. It is an important ingredient of Asian cuisine.

Specialist seed merchants and nurseries offer numerous forms of coriander specially selected for the production of seeds or leaves. For the wildlife-friendly garden seek out *C. s.* 'Moroccan', which produces flowers in preference to foliage and is one of the best varieties for attracting beneficial insects.

**Where to plant**

Coriander prefers fertile, well-drained soil and lots of light. Sow seed in a sunny area of the herb garden or in a large, well-drained patio pot in spring, about half an inch (1 cm) deep in finely raked soil.

**Caring for plants**

Coriander is susceptible to fungal wilt. To minimize the risk, thin out the seedlings to about 5 in. (13 cm) apart. Also make sure that the developing seedlings are watered well to prevent them from bolting.

Coriander is one of the plants most frequently visited by flower flies in the summer months.

# *Cornus* species and varieties

## Dogwood

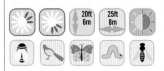

### Zones 5–9

Dogwoods are perfect small trees for wildlife. Although they can grow 20 ft. high and 25 ft. wide (6 x 8 m), many popular forms are half this size or even smaller, making them ideal specimens for small gardens. Conical in shape and with many horizontal branches often arranged in tiers, they provide good nesting sites for birds. The leaves emerge mid- or reddish green in spring and turn red-purple in fall before they are shed. For several weeks in spring to early summer the branches are covered with snowy white or pink blossoms, a rich source of nectar for bees and other pollinating insects. Although the clusters of bright red or blue-black fruit that follow are poisonous to humans, they are eaten by dozens of species of birds. Fruits are a favorite of fall migrants; any that remain are consumed in winter by woodpeckers, hermit thrushes and sparrows.

There are many cultivars in a range of shapes and sizes and with different colored flowers. Among the cultivars of *Cornus florida* are 'Cherokee Chief', which has dark ruby-pink flowers, 'Cloud Nine', with large, overlapping white flowers, and 'Pendula', which has a weeping habit. *C. f.* 'Rainbow', which has white flowers and yellow-edged, midgreen leaves turning red-purple in fall with prominent scarlet margins, is a compact, upright form, growing 10 x 8 ft. (3 x 2.5 m).

Many specialist nurseries also offer *C. kousa* x *C. florida* hybrids (sometimes listed as *C. x rutgersiensis*). These small, upright trees exhibit good resistance to dogwood anthracnose but are sterile and therefore do not produce fruit. They include *C.* 'Aurora' (syn. 'Rutban'), which has large, pure white flowers; *C.* 'Stellar Pink' (syn. 'Rutgan'), which has large, pink-flushed flowers that open creamy pink; and *C.* 'Ruth Ellen', an early-flowering variety more spreading in habit, which has white flowers maturing to pink.

The pagoda or alternate-leaf dogwood *Cornus alternifolia* 'Argentea' (which is sometimes offered as *C. a.* 'Variegata'), Zones 3–8, is a small shrub or tree with tiered branches of white-margined, bright green leaves and creamy white flowers in late spring to early summer, which are followed by spherical, blue-black fruit. It reaches 10 x 8 ft. (3 x 2.5 m) at maturity and is a lovely focal point in a woodland garden.

Forms of red-osier dogwood (*C. stolonifera*), Zones 2–7, are a valuable solution where there is insufficient space to plant a small tree. As well as providing nectar for insects and cover for birds, these clump-forming, deciduous shrubs with colored stems provide sustenance for the caterpillars of the Spring Azure butterfly. Selections include *C. s.* 'Flaviramea', which has white flowers in spring, followed by blue-tinged white fruits and dark green leaves that redden in autumn to reveal yellow-olive stems, and the compact *C. s.* 'Kelseyi', which has red-tipped, yellow-green winter stems and seldom exceeds 5 ft. (1.5 m).

*The fruits may cause a mild stomach upset if eaten.*

### Where to plant

Flowering dogwoods thrive in fertile, well-drained neutral to acidic soil in sun or light dappled shade. They are ideal specimens for a small garden or for creating an understory beneath something larger. Red-osier dogwood are best planted in small groups in sunny, moist areas of the garden, preferably near water.

### Caring for plants

Watch out for dogwood anthracnose, a potentially lethal fungal disease that thrives in cool, moist conditions. To minimize the risk, mulch around the base of the plant, water well weekly in dry spells and avoid damaging the base with your lawn mower or string trimmer.

Facing page: Dogwood blossoms are a cherished sign of spring in the southern United States.

# Cosmos bipinnatus

## Cosmos

### Zones 5–10

*Cosmos bipinnatus* is a nectar-rich, half-hardy annual that predator bugs find hard to resist. Flowering over a long period from early summer to midautumn, the large, open, saucer-shaped flowers, in shades of white, pink or crimson, offer a perfectly designed landing pad for insects and convenient access to the nectar. It is an easy annual to grow from seed, and the long, branching stems and feathery foliage are elegant additions to cut-flower arrangements.

Beneficial insects such as flower flies and lacewings appear to be particularly fond of white-flowered forms of cosmos, including the bushy, dwarf *C. b.* 'Sonata White', the crimson-edged, midborder *C. b.* 'Picotee' and the popular tall form, *C. b.* 'Purity'.

### Where to plant

Grow in a sunny spot in any reasonable, moist but well-drained soil. Avoid rich soils, which tend to encourage lush growth. Plant in drifts in a sunny border to fill gaps left by spring-flowering perennials and bulbs. The strong stems and reduced height of dwarf cosmos make them particularly suitable for use in windy sites such as roof gardens or balconies.

### Caring for plants

Protect young seedlings from slugs and snails with beer traps or eco-friendly pellets. Pinch out the growing tips to encourage the plant to develop a bushy habit, and stake tall varieties with ring-stakes or bamboo canes before the flowers appear. Deadhead regularly throughout summer to encourage new flowers. At the end of the season leave ripening seedheads on the plant to provide food for birds.

The long flowering season and filigree foliage make *Cosmos bipinnatus* one of the most valuable and attractive annuals.

# *Cotoneaster* cultivars and species

## Cotoneaster

### Zones 4–9

This large genus of hardy, berry-bearing shrubs includes many forms that are highly recommended for the wildlife-friendly garden. A dense tapestry of branches and small, lustrous, dark green leaves provides good nesting sites for small birds and homes to many of the insects on which they feed. In late spring and early summer the small, pinkish white or creamy-white flowers that are produced — singly or in clusters — are popular with honey bees and bumblebees. In autumn masses of small, jewel-like berries develop, sometimes against a backdrop of red or orange leaves. These are often retained for months, providing color and a source of food for birds in winter.

The branches of rock cotoneaster (*C. horizontalis*) form an attractive herringbone pattern. This compact, deciduous species, which bears pinkish white flowers followed by bright red berries, reaches a maximum of about 5 ft. (1.5 m) and is especially suitable for training against a sunny wall. The deciduous or semi-evergreen *C. simonsii* has pink-tinged white flowers followed by bright orange-red berries. This species grows 8 x 6 ft. (2.4 x 1.8 m) and produces a new set of leaves in midfall, which usually last until spring but may be shed before then in areas where winters are harsh. The strongly growing evergreen or semi-evergreen cultivar *C.* x *watereri* 'John Waterer' has white flowers followed by coral-red fruits, and the arching branches make it ideal for inclusion in a large shrub border.

*The seeds within cotoneaster berries may cause a mild stomach upset if eaten.*

### Where to plant

Cotoneasters will tolerate partial shade but produce considerably more fruit when they are growing in full sun. Renowned for their ability to survive in poor soils and exposed, windy conditions, they can be planted as a single specimen or as an informal, flowering hedge.

### Caring for plants

Once established, cotoneasters require little pruning. To minimize disruption to hibernating insects, remove congested, diseased or scantily clad branches in late winter or early spring, cutting cleanly back to the main stem.

*Cotoneaster atropurpureus* 'Variegatus' has white-margined leaves that turn pink and red in autumn.

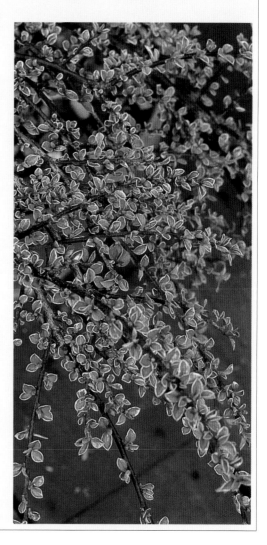

# *Crambe cordifolia*

## Giant sea kale

### Zones 3–9

Giant sea kale is a majestic, drought-tolerant, summer-flowering perennial, that is best reserved for large borders or gardens. In early and midsummer the billowing clouds of tiny, pure white, honey-scented flowers on open, branching stems — often reaching a yard (1 m) or more in diameter — are buzzing with bees. Caterpillars of the Cabbage White butterfly love to dine on the undersides of the colossal, crinkly, dark green leaves, so think carefully before deciding on a final site because the skeletonized leaves will look unsightly in a prominent position, and the deep taproot will make transplanting difficult once the plant is established.

For small gardens and borders sea kale (*C. maritima*), once a seasonal crop, may be a better choice. In early summer it produces clouds of honey-scented white flowers, held above handsomely ruffled, blue-green leaves.

### Where to plant

Giant sea kale is happiest in a sunny site with deep, fertile, well-drained soil. Use singly in a contemporary-style gravel garden with other bold foliage plants, or position toward the back of a large border, where any caterpillar damage to the leaves can be concealed. Like other members of the cabbage (brassica) family, sea kale prefers alkaline soil. If your soil is acidic, add a handful of ground limestone or dolomitic lime to the planting hole.

### Caring for plants

Cut back the faded flower stems and foliage in late autumn once the birds have had a few weeks to feed on the seed. Apply a generous mulch of well-rotted manure or garden compost around the crown. Although the old flower stems look wonderful frosted in the winter garden, don't refrain from cutting them back, because this can result in the plant failing to flower the following year.

Once established, *Crambe cordifolia* will tolerate dry conditions thanks to its long taproot.

# *Crocus tommasinianus*

## Tomasini's crocus

### Zones 4–8

This elegant species crocus starts blooming a full month before the blowsy Dutch crocuses that are commonly used in displays in public parks. On sunny days in late winter the slender, pale silvery lilac to deep reddish purple goblet-shaped flowers open to reveal glowing, bright orange stamens. These delicate blooms have all the qualities of a good late-winter bulb: they provide a rich source of nectar for bees emerging from hibernation and show an astonishing resilience to wind and rain. In addition to this, after flowering they die back gracefully, self-seeding freely and thereby guaranteeing an even more spectacular display the following year.

A number of hybrids are available, extending the color range and flowering season. *C. t.* var. *roseus* is a rare form with rose-pink to cyclamen-pink flowers; *C. t.* 'Whitewell Purple', which has reddish purple flowers, silvery-mauve inside, is a particularly fast-spreading form; *C. t.* 'Ruby Giant', which bears large, reddish purple flowers in early spring, spreads by forming offsets (unlike other varieties the seed of these is sterile).

If Tomasini's crocus is unavailable, the early-flowering Ankara crocus (*C. ancyrensis*), which has bright yellow or orange goblet-shaped blooms, is a good alternative.

### Where to plant

Like most winter- and spring-flowering bulbs, crocuses prefer a sunny site with gritty, well-drained soil. The bulbs are best planted in early to midautumn, 4 in. (10 cm) deep, in generous, naturalistic drifts. This effect is easily achieved by scattering a handful of bulbs at a time and planting them with a hand trowel or bulb-planter where they fall. To improve drainage around the roots, add a handful of coarse grit to the soil when planting in heavy clay.

### Caring for plants

Crocus bulbs are particularly attractive to small rodents, such as mice and voles. To prevent them from feasting on newly planted bulbs, carefully firm down the soil to conceal the planting holes. Where bulbs are naturalized in grass, delay cutting the lawn until after the leaves have finally died back.

*Crocus tommasinianus* is useful for naturalizing in difficult-to-manage areas of a sunny lawn or bank.

# Dianthus barbatus

## Sweet William

### Zones 3–9

Sweet William has been popular with gardeners since the early 16th century, and records show that a large consignment was purchased for King Henry VIII's garden at Hampton Court in England. Usually grown as biennials, these tidy, low-growing plants produce flattened heads of sweetly scented pink, purplish red or white flowers in late spring and early summer. Often bicolored with a well-defined pale center, the nectar-rich blooms are visited by many beneficial insects, including bees, butterflies, flower flies and parasitic mini-wasps.

Nurseries and garden centers often sell trays of sweet William in spring for use as summer bedding. The old-fashioned varieties are usually better for attracting butterflies because many of the newer cultivars do not have the spicy, clove-like scent to which the butterflies are drawn.

*D. barbatus* 'Auricula-eyed Mixed' produces heads of sweetly scented red, purple, rose or salmon-pink flowers, each with an attractive paler central eye. The plants in the *D. b.* Roundabout Series are bushy and compact and can be grown as annuals if sown early in the season. Producing a range of single and bicolored blooms on 8 in. (20 cm) stems, they are perfect for use in containers.

### Where to plant

Sweet William prefers a sunny spot with well-drained neutral to alkaline soil. It looks best planted in bold drifts at the front of a sunny cottage-style border. Alternatively, plant it near to an entrance or seating area where its scent can be fully appreciated.

### Caring for plants

Remove the first flush of spent blooms to prolong flowering but do not deadhead flowers borne later in the season in order to provide food for small birds and an opportunity for the plants to self-seed.

Sweet William flowers are popular with Swallowtail butterflies.

# *Digitalis purpurea*

## Common or purple foxglove

### Zones 4–9

The common or purple foxglove is particularly appealing to nectar-loving insects. Undoubtedly one of the bees' favorite-colored flowers, the maroon-spotted markings inside the tubular blooms highlight where the nectar is produced. The stately spikes satisfy the insects' sweet cravings from early to midsummer. In the right conditions, foxgloves perpetuate by self-seeding, sending up rosettes of hairy, dark green leaves to nourish emerging butterfly and moth larvae in spring.

*D. purpurea* f. *albiflora*, a naturally occurring pure white form of the common foxglove, is useful for illuminating shady or woodland areas of the garden.

*All parts of foxglove may cause severe discomfort if eaten. Contact with the foliage may irritate skin.*

### Where to plant

Grow foxglove in moist, humus-rich soil that does not dry out completely over summer. Plant in groups toward the back of the border or in a partially shady area of a woodland garden, with spring-blooming plants such as sweet rocket (*Hesperis matronalis*) and honesty (*Lunaria annua*).

### Caring for plants

Resist the urge to remove the spent flower spikes immediately after flowering. Left in place, they provide an opportunity for self-seeding and shelter for overwintering insects. Remove any unwanted self-sown seedlings in early spring and mulch with well-rotted organic matter.

The contrasting markings inside foxglove flowers are sophisticated signposts indicating where the nectar can be found.

# Dipsacus fullonum

## Teasel

| 5ft 1.5m | 32in 80cm |

### Zones 5–8

Nectar-loving insects are drawn in droves to the spiny, cone-shaped heads of teasel, an attractive biennial that is easily grown from seed. In midsummer the tightly packed flowerheads emerge on tall, upright stems from a prickly rosette of dark green leaves. The tiny lavender flowers open a few at a time, starting with a band at the middle of the cone and spreading to the opposite ends, guaranteeing a long flowering display. Small birds, especially goldfinches, love the brown seedheads, which persist well through winter. Other insect-eaters are sustained by the numerous insect casualties that drown in the water that collects at the base of the leaves.

Teasels provide food for both nectar-loving insects and birds.

### Where to plant

Teasels will grow in most moderately fertile soils, from neutral to alkaline. They are prolific self-seeders, so chose an area where you are happy for them to appear year after year. Used singly or in small groups, they make a striking architectural feature in a sunny border or wildlife garden.

### Caring for plants

To provide food for birds, leave the candelabra-like seedheads intact over the winter months. In spring cut back the faded flowerheads and foliage, and remove any unwanted self-sown seedlings.

*Note: listed as an invasive plant in Colorado and Iowa.*

# *Echinacea purpurea*

## Purple coneflower

### Zones 3–7

Purple coneflowers are among the most successful late-blooming perennials for attracting butterflies and bees. Between midsummer and early fall the large, mauve-crimson daisy-like flowers with orange-brown cone-shaped centers are a valuable source of nectar for insects preparing for hibernation. The stiff, branched stems stand up well to adverse weather conditions, providing structure and vertical interest in the winter garden while the seedheads are devoured by small birds.

Recommended cultivars include *E. p.* 'Magnus', a deep purple form with petals that are held almost horizontally, and the midborder *E. p.* 'White Swan', which has pure white petals and burnished orange-brown centers.

### Where to plant

Grow coneflowers in deep, well-drained, humus-rich soil. Attract butterflies by planting in groups toward the middle or back of a sunny border with other perennials that bloom in late summer, such as asters, black-eyed Susans (*Rudbeckia*) and yarrow (*Achillea*).

### Caring for plants

To encourage short, sturdy plants suitable for exposed, windy conditions, pinch back the growing tips in late spring. During summer, deadhead regularly to prolong flowering. To provide food for birds and shelter for overwintering insects, do not remove the faded flowerheads until the following spring. At the same time remove any unwanted self-sown seedlings and mulch with garden compost or well-rotted manure.

In North America renewed interest in purple coneflower has been influenced by the trend toward growing more native plants.

# *Echinops* cultivars

## Globe thistle

4ft 1.2m | 24in 60cm

**Zones 3–9**

Globe thistles are long-flowering perennials that attract pollinating insects and birds to the garden. In spring spiky, metallic or violet-blue flowerheads emerge on ghostly silver stems from clumps of prickly, gray-green leaves; from midsummer the spherical flowers receive frequent visits from butterflies and bees. As long as the plant is not cut back immediately after flowering, it continues to play an important role in supporting wildlife — many insects hibernate amid the spiky foliage, and the faded seedheads are popular with small birds, especially finches.

Generally, cultivated varieties of globe thistle are preferable to the species, many of which are potentially invasive. *E. bannaticus* 'Blue Globe', which has dark blue, spherical flowerheads, and *E. b.* 'Taplow Blue', which has violet-blue, spherical flowerheads, are relatively tall, growing to 4 ft. (1.2 m) high and 24 in. (60 cm) wide. *E. ritro* 'Veitch's Blue' is a remontant form, growing to 36 in. (90 cm) high, and is recommended for use as cut flowers. If globe thistle is cut back after flowering, it will produce a second flush of the metallic blue, spherical flowers on silvery branching stems.

### Where to plant

Globe thistles are undemanding plants. They will happily grow in poor soil as long as it is well drained, but they perform best in full sun. They look wonderful planted in generous clumps toward the back of a sunny mixed border, where they can be combined with later flowering plants to provide an alternative source of nectar once the flowers start to fade.

### Caring for plants

To provide shelter for hibernating insects and food for birds, do not remove the faded flowerheads. In early spring cut back what remains of the faded seedheads and foliage and remove any unwanted self-sown seedlings.

Globe thistles are more likely to attract butterflies if they are planted in generous clumps in a warm, sunny spot.

# *Elaeagnus* x *ebbingei*

## Elaeagnus

### Zones 6–9

These useful shrubs provide cover for many wildlife species and food when other sources are scarce. They are vigorous evergreen plants, which can grow to 12 ft. (4 m) tall and wide but which respond well to pruning, making them ideal for use as hedging. In late fall small, creamy white flowers fill the air with an exquisite sweet scent, reminiscent of gardenia, which attracts many late-flying bees. They are followed by small, bright red, football-like berries, 1 in. (2.5 cm) long by 0.5 in. (1 cm) wide, which ripen in midspring, long before other traditional early fruits. These are edible and prized by enthusiasts of permaculture, but the wildlife-friendly gardener will probably leave them to the birds.

In addition to the plain, dark-green-leaved hybrid, there are a number of ornamental cultivars, some of which produce reliable crops of fruit. One of the best is the variegated *E.* x *e.* 'Gilt Edge', which has golden-edged dark green leaves. It does best in full sun and is ideal for brightening large areas of dark green foliage. The cultivar *E.* x *e.* 'Salcombe Seedling' has similar leaves to the parent plant — metallic gray-green above, silvery underneath — but it flowers more freely and has a stronger scent.

*E. commutata* (Zones 2–6) is a medium-sized deciduous shrub with comparable wildlife uses. Native to North America, it forms dense thickets to 12 ft. (4 m) high and 6 ft. (1.8 m) wide, with reddish brown shoots and silvery-white leaves. The fragrant, yellowish white flowers, produced in the leaf axils in late spring, are followed by silvery, egg-shaped fruits about 0.3 in (8 mm) long. Ripening in early to midautumn, they will be eaten by many song- and gamebirds.

### Where to plant

As long as they are planted in well-drained soil, elaeagnus will grow almost anywhere, in full sun to deep shade. They can be planted singly or grouped to form an informal hedge. Their tolerance of salt-laden air makes them perfect for use as a windbreak in warm coastal areas.

### Caring for plants

To minimize disruption to overwintering insects and loss of food for birds, leave pruning until late spring, after the birds have finished foraging. Use secateurs to cut back any long or misplaced shoots and apply a generous mulch of well-rotted manure or compost around the base of the plant.

The tangled stems of *Elaeagnus* x *ebbingei* are an excellent nesting site for birds.

# *Eranthis hyemalis*

## Winter aconite

### Zones 4–9

Winter aconites, one of the earliest spring bulbs to bloom, are an important early source of nectar for bees emerging from winter hibernation. The bright yellow, buttercup-like flowers, each surrounded by a ruff of deeply divided, emerald-green leaves, open on mild winter days — often as early as midwinter, when there is still snow on the ground. They have a reputation for being difficult to cultivate, but this is usually because over-dried bulbs have been planted in an inappropriate site. For best results, plant tubers as soon as possible after purchase in a spot that remains moist over the summer months.

*All parts of this plant may cause severe discomfort if eaten. Contact with the foliage may irritate skin.*

### Where to plant

Grow in fertile, humus-rich, neutral to alkaline soil in direct sunlight or partial shade. In early or midautumn scatter generous groups of tubers in an informal pattern around the base of deciduous trees or shrubs in soil that does not dry out over summer. Wearing gloves, plant 2 in. (5 cm) deep and cover with soil. Winter aconites make wonderful companions for fragrant winter-flowering shrubs such as *Viburnum farreri* and winter honeysuckle (*Lonicera* x *purpusii*).

### Caring for plants

Lift and divide congested colonies of tubers in spring after flowering. Replant in small groups of four to six, taking care to position them at the depth at which they were originally growing.

Winter aconites purchased from specialist nurseries in spring generally establish better than dormant tubers.

# *Erysimum cheiri* (syn. *Cheiranthus cheiri*)

## English wallflower

### Zones 7–10

English wallflowers are a rich source of nectar for early-flying insects, including butterflies and bees. Usually grown as biennials, these hardy evergreen plants produce clusters of primrose-yellow, orange, scarlet or cream flowers that fill the spring garden with a delicious sweet scent and make long-lasting cut flowers. In large, formal displays wallflowers are usually replaced as soon as they have finished flowering, but a wildlife-friendly gardener will probably choose to leave them to go to seed to provide a food source for birds.

Wallflowers are often sold bare-rooted at farmers' markets in the fall, ready for planting in their final flowering position. If you prefer to grow them from seed, choose one of the ordinary bedding varieties, which tend to be more strongly scented and attractive to pollinators than cultivars such as *E.* 'Bowles' Mauve', which are grown as perennials. The *E. c.* Bedder Series are sturdy compact plants growing to 12 in. (30 cm) high, ideal for use in containers. For cutting, choose one of the taller varieties, such as *E. c.* 'Blood Red', which as the name suggests has blood-red flowers and 15 in. (38 cm) stems.

### Where to plant

English wallflowers do best in moderately fertile, well-drained soil. They are in the same family as cabbages, and you may need to add extra lime to the soil to discourage clubroot. Traditionally raised from seed sown outdoors in spring and transplanted to their final positions in autumn, they look great massed in a sunny border or large container, underplanted with single-flowered tulips.

### Caring for plants

Wallflower leaves are often damaged by caterpillars and flea beetles. To minimize unsightly caterpillar damage check the undersides of the foliage regularly in summer and early fall. Pick off any insects feeding on plants in prominent positions and put them on the leaves of another, less conspicuous plant.

Wallflowers are one of the favorite food plants of the Cabbage White butterfly. The adult butterflies obtain nectar from the flowers while the caterpillars feed on the leaves.

# *Eschscholzia californica*

## California poppy

### Zones 8–10

California poppies are good for attracting pollinating insects to difficult-to-cultivate areas of the garden. Throughout summer they produce masses of single, cup-shaped flowers, 2 to 3 in. (5 to 8 cm) across, above mounds of finely divided bluish green leaves. The silky petals are predominantly golden-orange, yellow or white — the colors that flower flies and other beneficial insects find particularly alluring. Both heat- and drought-tolerant, they close at night and on dull days when light levels are low. After they have finished flowering, they self-seed freely, guaranteeing food for birds and plants in the border for the following year.

When you are choosing one of the many cultivated forms of California poppies offered by seed merchants try to find single-flowered forms, such as *E. c.* 'Alba', which has lovely creamy white flowers, and *E. c.* 'Inferno', which has glowing orange-scarlet flowers. These afford insects easy access to the pollen.

### Where to plant

California poppies are easily grown from seed sown in early autumn or midspring. Because they dislike root disturbance, they are best sown where they are to flower, in poor, well-drained soil and full sun. They look great growing in generous drifts with other low-growing annuals or underplanted among silver-leaved perennials, such as artemisia.

### Caring for plants

In summer deadhead regularly to prolong flowering. At the end of the season leave the ripening seedheads in place to provide food for birds and a chance for the plant to self-seed.

California poppies produce many self-sown seedlings. You can transplant them while they are still small, as long as care is taken not to disturb the roots.

# *Eupatorium* species and cultivars

## Joe Pye weed, hemp agrimony

### Zones 3–9

Joe Pye weed is a majestic summer-flowering perennial, loved by butterflies, birds and bees. Often reaching more than 6 ft. (1.8 m) tall, large plants bear umbrella-like heads of pink, purple or white flowers on upright stems from midsummer to early autumn. The self-supporting, cane-like stems are covered with whorls of finely toothed leaves, which release a scent of vanilla when crushed. As well as some of the most common butterflies — including the Painted Lady, Monarch and Red Admiral — the nectar-rich blooms attract other small insects, which in turn provide food for birds.

At 7 ft. (2.2 m) tall, *E. purpureum*, with pink-purple or creamy white flowers on purple-tinted stems, is one of the best varieties for attracting butterflies. *E. p.* subsp. *maculatum* 'Atropurpureum' has rose-purple flowers and deep purple stems to 5 ft. (1.5 m) tall. The late-blooming *E. p.* 'Purple Bush', which has mauve flowers on purple stems in late summer to midautumn, grows to about 36 in. (90 cm) tall and is particularly suitable for small gardens. *E. cannabinum* (hemp agrimony) produces flat-topped heads of pink, mauve or white flowers on red-tinted stems to 5 ft. (1.5 m) tall.

### Where to plant

Eupatoriums prefer fertile, slightly alkaline soil but will happily grow in a range of conditions, as long as they receive adequate moisture. To encourage butterflies, plant in bold clumps in a sunny spot, toward the back of the border or in a boggy area close to a pond or stream.

### Caring for plants

Make sure that the fibrous roots do not dry out by applying a generous mulch of garden compost or well-rotted manure around the crowns of the plants in spring, and water well during prolonged dry spells.

The umbrella-like flowers of *Eupatorium* offer an ideal landing platform for butterflies.

# Filipendula ulmaria

## Meadowsweet, queen of the meadows

### Zones 3–8

Meadowsweet is a moisture-loving perennial that is favored by many insect pollinators, including moths, flower flies and solitary bees. In summer fluffy plumes of tiny, honey-scented, creamy white flowers appear on slender, upright stems above clumps of deeply divided, dark green leaves. This is an invaluable plant for boggy areas of a "moonlit garden" designed to attract nectar-feeding moths and bats, and in early winter the faded flowerheads are foraged by seed-eating birds and small mammals in search of food.

Both *F. u.* 'Variegata', with cream-splashed, dark green leaves and creamy white flowers, and *F. u.* 'Aurea', which has golden-yellow leaves, are useful for illuminating a shady spot. The North American native species, *F. rubra*, has billowing clusters of deep peach-pink flowers on red branching stems, followed by reddish fruits, and it can grow to 8 ft. (2.4 m) tall, earning it the name queen of the prairie. This and the popular form *F. r.* 'Venusta', which has deep rose-pink flowers that become paler with age, work best in a large or medium-sized site.

### Where to plant

Meadowsweet prefers fertile, moist but well-drained soil and partial shade. Use in bold swaths around the moist margins of a wildlife pond or in boggy areas of a woodland garden.

### Caring for plants

To provide food for birds and shelter for overwintering insects, do not remove the faded flowerheads and foliage until the following spring. Mildew may be a problem if insufficient nutrients and moisture are available at the roots. To help prevent mildew from taking hold apply a generous mulch of well-rotted leaf mold around the base of plants in spring.

*Filipendulina rubra* is particularly suitable for a prairie-style planting.

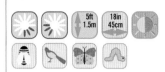

# *Gaura lindheimeri*

## White gaura

### Zones 5–9

White gaura has been enjoying a resurgence of interest in recent years, partly because of its use in the "new perennial" style of planting that has become popular in North America and Europe. From early summer until the first frosts the plant produces a succession of small, white, star-shaped flowers, held high above the foliage on slender wiry stems. The ephemeral blooms, which open a few at a time at dawn and fade to pink before they are shed, are popular with butterflies and bees. Once established, white gaura is heat- and drought-tolerant and has the added advantage of looking attractive after it has finished flowering.

Although the plant can grow up to 5 ft. (1.5 m) high with a spread of 36 in. (90 cm), some of the cultivars that have been developed are more compact. *G. l.* 'Corrie's Gold' sends up showers of pink-white star-shaped flowers on 30 in. (75 cm) stems above clumps of gold-margined leaves. Similar in size, *G. l.* 'Whirling Butterflies' is a particularly free-flowering form with white star-shaped flowers and red sepals.

### Where to plant

White gaura performs best in well-drained, fertile soil in a warm, sunny spot. Plant singly or in small groups, allowing at least 3 to 4 ft. (1 to 1.2 m) between plants, which are difficult to transplant once established. Water well and apply a deep mulch.

### Caring for plants

Established plants will tolerate infrequent watering, thanks to their deep taproots. Resist the temptation to cut the plant back after it has finished flowering, because the foliage takes on beautiful autumn tints, particularly in cold spells, and provides some shelter for overwintering insects.

Gaura is an important food plant for many rare native North American butterflies and moths, populations of which have been reduced by the widespread use of pesticides and biological controls to control infestations of more troublesome insect pests.

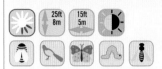

# *Hedera helix* cultivars

## Common ivy, English ivy

[ 25ft 8m ] [ 15ft 5m ]

### Zones 5–9

Ivy has a justifiable reputation as one of the best wildlife-friendly evergreen climbers. It is one of the favorite larval food plants of the little Holly Blue butterfly, whose autumn-born brood of caterpillars feeds off the emerging buds while the lustrous, lobed, dark green leaves provide refuge for overwintering chrysalises. Initially slow-growing, established specimens develop a dense, woody framework that small birds love to nest in. On mature plants clusters of yellowish green autumn flowers, an important late-autumn source of nectar, are followed by spherical black fruit, which are devoured in winter by birds.

*Hedera helix* cultivars offer a wide range of attractively shaped and variegated foliage. *H. h.* 'Oro di Bogliasco' (syn. 'Goldheart') is a vigorous, variegated form with a distinctive golden-yellow center; it does equally well in sun or partial shade. *H. h.* var. *baltica*, which has dark green leaves with contrasting veins that turn purple in winter, is ideal for use as groundcover in shady areas of the garden.

*H. h.* 'Thorndale' has similar though slightly larger leaves than *H. h.* var. *baltica*. Reliably hardy to Zone 4, it is one of the best cold-hardy forms of ivy.

*All parts of ivy may cause severe discomfort if eaten. Contact with the sap may irritate skin.*

### Where to plant

Grow in fertile, moist, well-drained soil, preferably alkaline. Use singly or in groups as groundcover or to provide cover for a wire topiary structure, wall or fence. Because ivy prefers alkaline soil, it's perfect for planting areas recently cleared of builders' rubble.

### Caring for plants

Although pruning can be carried out at any time of the year, to minimize disruption to overwintering insects and nesting birds it's best undertaken in late spring or early summer.

*Hedera helix* 'Goldchild' is a compact variegated form that is ideal for illuminating a low garden wall.

# *Helianthus annuus* cultivars

## Sunflower

### Zones 1–11

Sunflowers need little introduction. Many adults will have taken their first, tentative steps into gardening by growing them when they were children. Seed sown outdoors from spring to early summer will produce large, daisy-like flowers, often with a darker, contrasting center, on stout, upright stems. From midsummer to early autumn the spectacular blooms are visited by bees and many species of butterfly, including the Monarch, Red Admiral and Painted Lady. As temperatures start to fall and the flowers run to seed they are stripped from their individual compartments by goldfinches and other seed-eating birds.

Annual sunflowers have been hybridized to produce myriad colors, heights and flowering forms. *H. a.* 'Velvet Queen' is a multiheaded form bearing sumptuous, deep velvet-red to copper-colored daisy-like flowers on stems to 6 ft. (1.8 m) tall. With rich orange-yellow flowers the size of dinner plates on stems to 10 ft. (3 m) tall, the aptly named *H. a.* 'Russian Giant' is one of the largest and tallest sunflowers currently available. *H. a.* 'Taiyo', a tall, single-stemmed sunflower with rich orange-yellow petals, is great for use indoors. For fans of white flowers there's even a creamy white cultivar, *H. a.* 'Italian White'.

*Contact with the foliage may aggravate skin allergies.*

### Where to plant

Grow sunflowers in moderately fertile, moist but well-drained soil in full sun. Sow seeds outdoors from early spring to early summer where they are to flower in soil raked to a fine tilth. Sunflowers are useful for adding height and interest to a sunny border or for creating an unusual temporary flowering screen.

*Helianthus* 'Lemon Queen' produces masses of lemon-yellow daisy-like flowers on branching stems.

### Caring for plants

Once the seedlings are established, feed each week with a balanced liquid fertilizer. The large, tall cultivars that develop stems as thick as walking-sticks need support early on with hardwood stakes driven into the ground with a sledgehammer. To provide food for small birds leave the seedheads intact until spring.

# Heliotropium arborescens

## Heliotrope, cherry pie

**Zones 9–11**

Heliotrope is a fragrant, long-flowering shrub, originally from Peru. It is usually treated as a half-hardy annual by gardeners in the northern hemisphere and can be easily grown from seed sown indoors in early spring. Plants produce tightly packed spikes of tiny, tubular dark violet, lavender-blue or white flowers and handsomely wrinkled and veined dark green leaves. The tiny flowers open gradually through summer, providing a nonstop source of nectar for butterflies and bees. Although traditionally used as summer bedding, heliotrope is particularly effective in a windowbox, wall-mounted container or hanging basket, where the sweetly scented flowers can be appreciated close up.

*H. a.* 'Marine' is a compact bushy form, growing to about 18 in. (45 cm) high, which produces heads 6 in. (15 cm) across of tightly packed, dark violet-blue flowers. *H. a.* 'Mini Marine', a dwarf form of *H. a.* 'Marine', grows to 16 in. (40 cm) tall and wide and is perfect for growing in containers.

*Contact with the foliage may cause both skin and eye irritation.*

### Where to plant

Heliotrope grows best in direct sunlight and in a position where it receives some protection from cold, drying winds. Ideally, grow it where it will receive sun in the morning but some shade later in the day. It can be grown singly or in groups to create a perfumed summer display.

### Caring for plants

As heliotrope seedlings mature, pinch back the growing tips to encourage bushy growth and do not plant outdoors until all risk of frost has passed. Water well during the growing season and feed with a balanced liquid fertilizer once a month. In early autumn bring container-grown plants indoors or take cuttings from the stem tips to start new plants over winter.

Butterflies are attracted by heliotrope's vibrant flowers and unusual fragrance, said by many to be reminiscent of the smell of freshly baked cherry pie.

# *Humulus lupulus*

## Hop

### Zones 3–8

Planting an ornamental hop is one of the quickest ways of providing shelter and food for wildlife. After its winter dormancy, this twining vine grows at a prolific rate — often as much as 20 ft. (6 m) in a single season. Hops are a favorite host plant of the Question Mark and Eastern Comma butterflies, and in spring their spiny offspring love to dine on the undersides of the toothed, maple-like leaves. For the full ornamental effect buy a female plant from a reputable grower. Male plants are fine for foliage, but only females will produce the pale green to straw-colored, cone-like fruits that festoon the vine in early fall.

The attractive golden-leaved form, *H. l.* 'Aureus', has lime-green leaves and greenish yellow flowers, and it makes a fabulous background for a late-blooming clematis, such as *Clematis* 'Etoile Violette'.

### Where to plant

Hops prefer to spread their roots in deep, fertile, well-drained soil. For the best topgrowth and foliage color chose a sunny site, especially for the golden-leaved form, whose foliage remains resolutely light green if grown in shade. Hops are perfect for screening a fence or wall or for growing through a strong tree. To encourage sturdy, upward growth use a network of galvanized wires, tying young shoots to them with soft garden twine as they develop.

### Caring for plants

To provide shelter for overwintering insects, delay cutting back the faded foliage and flowers until early spring. So that powdery mildew doesn't take hold, avoid planting hops in dry, sandy soils; always mulch them generously after pruning and water well during prolonged hot, dry spells.

Small birds often use the dried fruits of ornamental hops as nesting material.

# *Hyssopus officinalis*

## Hyssop

### Zones 3–9

Hyssop is one of the best herbs to plant if you need help with the pollination of home-grown vegetables or fruit. Easily raised from seed or division, this bushy, semi-evergreen shrub produces slender, upright spikes of nectar-rich, dark blue, pink or white flowers from early summer to midfall. As well as being an important butterfly and bee attractant, the herb's strong aroma is said to reduce damage caused by the Cabbage White butterfly by masking the smell of nearby brassica crops.

In addition to the traditional blue-flowered form, which grows to about 24 in. (60 cm) high, a white-flowered form, *H. o.* f. *albus*, and a pink-flowered form, *H. o.* 'Roseus', are readily available. Rock hyssop (*H. o.* subsp. *aristatus*), a dwarf selection with blue flowers, is particularly suitable for growing in a container.

### Where to plant

Hyssop prefers a sunny spot and light, well-drained, slightly alkaline soil. It is often used to edge a vegetable garden or *potager* or for filling in spaces among taller perennials.

### Caring for plants

To minimize disruption to hibernating insects, delay pruning hyssop until early spring, when the stems can be cut back hard almost to ground level. Specimens grown as hedging should be lightly clipped in early or midspring to remove any top leaves that have become brown and wilted.

For centuries beekeepers have planted hyssop near their hives, knowing how much bees love the plant's nectar-rich flowers.

# *Ilex* cultivars

## Holly

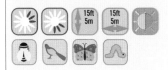

### Zones 5–8

Female fruiting forms of holly, which provide both shelter and food, are among the most valuable shrubs and trees that the wildlife-friendly gardener can grow. An important host plant of the Holly Blue butterfly, its spring-born brood of caterpillars will feed on the lustrous, light-reflecting spiny leaves, while adult butterflies develop a taste for the nectar of the inconspicuous, white spring flowers. An abundant crop of scarlet or yellow autumn berries is guaranteed as long as a male form of holly is planted close by for every three to five female plants. Often persisting through most of the winter, the fruits provide essential cold-weather food for dozens of species of songbirds.

Deciduous varieties with persistent bright red fruits include *I.* 'Sparkleberry', which has toothed, dark green leaves that are retained until early winter, and *I. verticillata* 'Winter Red', which has dark green, toothed foliage with long, sharply pointed tips. Meserve holly hybrids are particularly useful for their cold-hardiness and tolerance of heat. *I.* x *meserveae* 'Blue Princess' has large, softly spiny bluish green leaves on purple-green stems; *I.* x *meserveae* 'China Girl' has bright green foliage and chartreuse stems.

*Holly berries may cause a mild stomach upset if eaten.*

### Where to plant

Grow hollies in moist but well-drained, moderately fertile, humus-rich soil in sun or partial shade. Variegated forms produce the best color in full sun. Holly is incredibly versatile: it can be used as a spectacular four-seasons specimen tree, grown as a fruiting hedge or trained into numerous topiary shapes.

### Caring for plants

Freestanding specimens require minimal pruning — simply remove diseased or misplaced branches in spring. Trim plants that are grown as hedges in late summer, taking care that cuts are made above the developing berries. After pruning remember to apply a generous mulch of compost or well-rotted manure around the base.

Plants like this variegated box-leaved holly, *Ilex crenata* 'Variegata', are ideal for city gardens as they are tolerant of pollution and cope well with the shade cast by tall buildings.

# Jasminum officinale

## Common jasmine, poet's jasmine

### Zones 7-11

Jasmine is a justifiably popular vine. The scent of a single specimen can perfume an entire garden, pervading adjacent sidewalks and neighbouring properties. It quickly spreads in all directions, forming a densely tangled mass of twining stems and slender mid-green leaflets – providing a haven for insects and nesting birds. The plant produces a succession of white or pink-tinted, star-shaped, jasmine-scented flowers from early summer to early fall. These attract butterflies and bees by day, and after dark, the flowers' heady scent and light-reflecting petals attract night-time pollinators.

  *J. o.* f. *affine* has pink-edged, white flowers up to 1. 5 in. (4 cm) across – twice the size of those of the species. *J. o.* 'Argenteovariegatum' (syn. *J. o* 'Variegatum') has white-margined grey-green leaves and pure-white flowers. The golden-variegated form, *J. o.* 'Aureum', has mid-green leaves with conspicuous yellow markings and white flowers. *J. o.* 'Fiona Sunrise' (syn. *J. o.* 'Frojas') has golden-yellow foliage and small white flowers from late spring to early fall and is more compact than other varieties, reaching a height and spread of 10 ft. (3 m) in 10 years.

### Where to plant

Jasmine is easily grown in most fertile, well-drained garden soils and performs best in a sheltered sunny position. It is ideal for covering a large south or west-facing wall, an unsightly garden structure or bare chain-link fence. The variegated forms are particularly valuable for illuminating gloomy corners of your garden.

### Caring for plants

Young specimens require minimal pruning. Treat established specimens immediately after the flowers have faded, removing old or over-crowded stems. Afterwards apply a mulch of compost or well-rotted manure around the base.

After dark the pure-white, star-shaped flowers of *Jasminum officinale* (common jasmine) attract nocturnal pollinators, such as Sphinx and Hawk moths.

# Juncus effusus

## Soft rush

### Zones 4–9

Soft rush is an excellent starter plant if you want to attract young frogs, dragonflies and water birds to a pond. Although the tiny, terminal clusters of brown flowers that appear in summer won't win any show prizes, the spiky, dark green cylindrical stems have numerous attractions for wildlife. Planted around the shallow margins of a pond, they offer a refuge for amphibians and small water birds and, perhaps best of all, on sunny days mating dragonflies seem to find the needle-like foliage a particularly convivial place to perform their acrobatic antics.

Corkscrew rush (*J. e.* f. *spiralis*), a low-growing relative, has tightly curled, dark green leafless stems, which become more tangled and curly over time. Although less important in terms of wildlife, its curious corkscrew-like stems are guaranteed to be a talking point.

### Where to plant

Soft rush is easily grown in water that is less than 3 in. (8 cm) deep or in permanently moist, acidic soil. Although it does best in partial shade, it will tolerate full sun as long as the roots are not deprived of moisture. To provide maximum cover for wildlife, plant in generous clumps around the margins of a pond, with broad-leaved bog plants that offer contrasting foliage, such as yellow skunk cabbage (*Lysichiton americanus*). Soft rush may be easily grown in a miniature bog garden on a balcony or roof garden. It's possible to create this type of micro habitat in a wooden half-barrel or an old ceramic sink. Always check first that the load-bearing capacity of the balcony or roof is sufficient to support the weight.

### Caring for plants

Rejuvenate congested clumps of soft rush from midspring to early summer. Leave discarded parts of the plant next to the pool for several days so that any small creatures sheltering in the foliage can re-enter the water.

Damselflies and dragonflies love to perch on the tapering, strongly upright stems of soft rush.

# *Knautia* species

## Knautia

5ft 1.5m 12in 30cm

### Zones 5–8

Knautia are hardy, summer-flowering perennials loved by pollinating insects and birds. In midsummer plants send up slender branching stems that bear masses of pin-cushion-like flowers from rosettes of narrow or deeply divided midgreen leaves. Often putting on a nonstop display until the first frosts, the dainty flowers have ultraviolet marks on the petals that draw butterflies and bees. Though not visible to the human eye, these form a checkered pattern that directs the insects to the nectar. After knautia have finished flowering, the fuzzy brown seedheads provide fall interest in gardens and are popular with seed-eating birds.

Field scabious (*K. arvensis* syn. *Scabious rumelica*) is a tall plant, growing to 5 ft. (1.5 m), and its bluish lilac flowerheads, to 1.5 in. (4 cm) across, are popular with many common butterflies, including the Painted Lady and Red Admiral. *K. macedonica* is smaller, reaching 32 in. (80 cm) tall and 18 in. (45 cm) across.

### Where to plant

Knautia thrive in well-drained, alkaline soil in full sun. Field scabious is an excellent choice for a wildflower meadow, while the shorter *K. macedonica* is perfect for the front of a mixed or herbaceous border.

### Caring for plants

In prolonged periods of wet weather or in rich soils knautia has a tendency to flop over untidily. To prevent it from sprawling over other plants, support it with a framework of twigs or brushwood before the flowers appear. Do not cut back the faded flowerheads and stems until early spring to provide food for birds and a place for insects to hibernate. Unwanted self-sown seedlings can be removed at the same time.

The deep crimson flowerheads of *Knautia macedonica* bring long-lasting color to the late-summer garden.

# Lathyrus odoratus

## Sweet pea

### Zones 3–9

Plant old-fashioned heirloom varieties of sweet peas to help in the pollination of home-grown vegetables or fruit. These hardy annual vines grow to 6 ft. (1.8 m) tall, attaching themselves to the nearest support by means of wispy tendrils. Over a long period in summer to early autumn they produce masses of wavy-edged, single-or bicolored blooms. Although the flowers are smaller and fewer on each stem than on those of more recent hybrids, the exquisite scent of the older cultivars is highly attractive to pollinating insects, such as butterflies and bees.

The resurgence in interest in old-fashioned sweet peas has encouraged many seed merchants to offer a good selection of colors, from the purple and blue bicolored blooms of the original sweet pea to pure white.

*L. o.* 'Cupani', which has small, purple and dark blue bicolored flowers, is named after the priest who found it growing wild in Sicily in 1695. It bears two flowers on each stem with bushy plants that rarely grow more than 3 to 4 ft. (1 to 1.2 m) high. More recent in origin, *L. o.* 'Matucana' produces four relatively large, bicolored maroon and violet flowers on plants growing to 5 ft. (1.5 m) high. The cultivar *L. o.* 'Dorothy Eckford' bears three elegant, pure white flowers on a stem, while *L. o.* 'Lord Nelson' has dark blue, almost navy blue flowers with an intoxicating spicy fragrance. *L. o.* 'Painted Lady', which has three or four dark rose-pink and white bicolored blooms on a stem, dates from the 18th century. In warm zones *L. o.* 'Queen Alexandra', with three scarlet blooms on a stem, is popular with hummingbirds. Unlike other scarlet-flowered cultivars, 'Queen Alexandra' holds its color well, even in strong sunlight.

*All parts of* Lathyrus odoratus *are poisonous.*

### Where to plant

Sweet peas are usually grown up a wigwam of bamboo canes or pollarded hazel in a sunny spot. To encourage germination, soak the seeds for 24 hours and nick the hard outer coating with a sharp knife before planting. Sweet peas dislike root disturbance, so it is a good idea to sow the pre-soaked seeds directly in fertile, well-drained soil in groups of three around each of the supports.

### Caring for plants

When the plantlets are 6 in. (15 cm) high, pinch out the shoot tips to encourage bushy growth, and mulch with well-rotted compost to keep the roots cool and help retain moisture in the soil. To prolong flowering water regularly, applying a liquid fertilizer every two weeks, and remember to cut the flowers as they appear to prevent seeds from forming.

The small petals of old-fashioned varieties of sweet pea are strong enough to allow bumblebees to perch comfortably while they are sipping nectar from the base of the flower.

# *Lavandula* cultivars

## Lavender

### Zones 5–9

Planting a hedge of lavender or even a single specimen in a pot is a great way of supporting pollinating insects and birds. Best planted in fall or early spring, these compact evergreen plants have silver-gray or gray-green leaves that release a wonderful, refreshing aroma when touched. From midsummer to early autumn they send up scented spikes of pale to dark purple, lavender, violet-blue or pinkish white flowers on slender, unbranched stems. The fresh flowers are a good source of nectar for butterflies, bees and moths, and the dry flower-heads are a popular foraging food for birds.

There are dozens of winter-hardy lavenders, offering the gardener a range of different flower colors, plant forms and garden uses.

Indisputably the best English lavender for edging paths and borders is the compact and bushy *Lavandula angustifolia* 'Hidcote', which has dark violet flowers and silver-gray leaves. A dwarf form, *L. a.* 'Lady', has soft blue flowers and gray-green leaves and rarely grows more than 12 in. (30 cm) high and wide, making it ideal for a sunny windowbox or patio container. *L. a.* 'Munstead', with blue-purple flowers and gray-green leaves, is a good choice for a low hedge, since it grows only 18 to 24 in. (45 to 60 cm). *L. a.* 'Royal Purple' is a majestic form with rich purple-blue flowers on long, slender stems and gray-green, aromatic leaves. Later flowering than the English lavenders, *L.* x *intermedia* 'Grosso' is one of the best varieties for a wildlife garden — its fat purple-violet flower spikes are a magnet for bees and other nectar-loving insects. A wilt-resistant variety developed in France, it is perfect for hot, southern gardens.

### Where to plant

Lavenders prefer full sun and well-drained soil. Versatile and easy-to-grow, they can be planted as a single specimen or massed to form a fragrant flowering edge to a sunny path or border.

### Caring for plants

To provide food for small birds and a place for hibernating insects, delay removing the old flowering stalks until early or midspring. Then cut back the flowered shoots to within 1 in. (2.5 cm) of the old growth, taking care not to cut into the old wood, which will not regenerate.

Lavenders are a good wildlife-friendly choice where space is limited, because they can be easily grown in containers.

# Liatris spicata

## Gayfeather, blazing star

**Zones 4–9**

Gayfeather is a long-flowering, drought-tolerant perennial, valued equally by wildlife gardeners and dried-flower arrangers. The species is native to damp areas of Eastern North America, and between midsummer and early autumn the strongly upright fluffy spikes are a favorite source of nectar for bees, rare moths and butterflies. The purple, pink or white flowers open from the top down — a characteristic that makes them excellent for use as dried flowers because the top is usually the most visible part of the display. As long as the plant is not cut back prematurely, in late autumn and early winter you will often see small birds, such as finches, clinging to the dried, blackened flower spikes in search of the feathery seeds.

Although the species commonly grows to 6 ft. (1.8 m) tall in the wild, cultivated forms are more compact. *L. s.* 'Floristan Weiss', which produces white, bottlebrush-like spikes, grows to 36 in. (90 cm) tall, and *L. s.* 'Kobold', which has bright purplish pink flowers and is one of the most commonly available purple forms, rarely exceeds 24 in. (60 cm).

### Where to plant

Grow gayfeather in fertile, reliably moist but well-drained soil. Choose a sunny spot with plenty of space for air to circulate around the stems because gayfeather is susceptible to powdery mildew if it is overcrowded or grown in shade.

### Caring for plants

Protect the leaves from slug and snail damage by using beer traps or eco-friendly pellets. To provide food for small birds, do not cut back the blackened flower spikes until early spring. Congested colonies can also be lifted and divided at this time every three or four years.

Used fresh or dried, gayfeather blooms make exceptionally long-lasting cut flowers.

# *Limnanthes douglasii*

## Poached egg plant, Douglas's meadowfoam

### Zones 7–11

The poached egg plant is one of the most valuable hardy annuals to grow if you want to keep unwanted pests at bay without using harmful chemicals. Seed sown in early spring or autumn quickly produces a low carpet of fern-like, bright yellow-green leaves, covered in summer and early autumn with fragrant saucer-shaped, yellow-centered white flowers. The nectar-rich blooms are sought out by flower flies and bees.

*L. d.* var. *sulphurea* is a pretty, pale yellow form sold by specialist seed merchants.

Seed can be sown in autumn to provide a weed-suppressing green manure on those parts of the vegetable garden that would be otherwise vacant. Dig in the leafy growth in spring before planting other crops.

### Where to plant

Grow in fertile, moist, well-drained soil. Poached egg plants are ideal for growing in a pot, for planting near ornamental or food crops that are affected by aphids or for edging a sunny annual border.

### Caring for plants

Sow seeds in early spring or early autumn in soil raked to a fine tilth. In areas subject to frost protect autumn-sown seedlings with a glass, polycarbonate or plastic cloche. As part of routine border maintenance in spring, remove faded foliage along with any unwanted self-sown seedlings. Deadhead regularly to extend the flowering season.

As well as attracting beneficial insects and pollinators, the poached egg plant is excellent for suppressing weeds.

# Lobelia cardinalis

## Cardinal flower

### Zones 3–9

The cardinal flower is a spectacular, but short-lived, summer- and fall-flowering perennial loved by insects and birds. From late summer on, spikes of bright scarlet-red flowers appear on beet-red stained stems clothed with slender bright green or bronze-tinted leaves. In warm zones the showy, tubular flowers attract hummingbirds, whose long tongues are perfectly designed to reach the sugary nectar at the base of each bloom. This lobelia is best grown in moist or even wet soil, and where winters are mild the foliage remains intact. Because winter sun is key to the plant's survival, it is important to prevent fallen leaves and plant debris from smothering the crown.

Cardinal flower cultivars include *L.* 'Cherry Ripe', which has cherry-red flowers set against midgreen or occasionally maroon-tinted leaves, and one of the oldest hybrids, *L.* 'Queen Victoria', which has scarlet flowers and deep purple-red foliage.

*All parts of the cardinal flower are poisonous. Contact with the sap may cause skin irritation.*

### Where to plant

Grow in deep, fertile, reliably moist soil in sun or dappled shade. Cardinal flowers are ideal for planting in drifts along the moist margins of a stream or wildlife pond or for filling gaps left in the border by early-flowering perennials.

### Caring for plants

To provide food for seed-eating birds, do not cut back the faded flower spikes until the following spring. In frost-prone areas protect the crown with a light, dry mulch held in place with chicken wire. To rejuvenate large, congested clumps, lift and divide plants every second spring.

The cardinal flower is one of the favorite plants of the Ruby-throated hummingbird.

# *Lonicera sempervirens*

## Coral honeysuckle, trumpet honeysuckle

**Zones 4–9**

Coral honeysuckle is a summer-blooming twining vine, valued by nectar-loving insects and birds. From early summer to early fall whorls of unscented, scarlet-orange, trumpet-shaped flowers with coppery-orange throats are produced at the ends of flowering shoots. In warm zones hummingbirds are drawn to the showy flowers to sip the nectar. The small, translucent red berries that follow in hot summers are relished by several common species of songbirds, including the American goldfinch and robin.

Unlike other species of *Lonicera*, which can be invasive, coral honeysuckle won't get out of control and end up strangling your favorite shrubs. When it is planted in a sunny, sheltered spot, its handsomely paired leaves offer valuable nesting cover and shelter for insects.

Scarlet trumpet honeysuckle (*L.* x *brownii*), a hybrid of *L. sempervirens* and *L. hirsuta*, has lightly scented, orange-red flowers and bluish green leaves. Reliably hardy in Zones 3 to 6, it is particularly suitable for use as groundcover. *L.* x *b.* 'Dropmore Scarlet' produces long, trumpet-shaped scarlet flowers over a long period from midsummer.

**Where to plant**

If it is do to well, coral honeysuckle must have a consistently moist, neutral to slightly acidic soil and a south- or southwest-facing site. Ideal for covering a pergola, fence or wall, the twining stems should be tied against trellis or galvanized wires until they are well established.

**Caring for plants**

Like its spring-flowering cousins, coral honeysuckle is susceptible to blackfly, and spraying with a mixture of water and liquid soap is a good way to cope with major infestations. To provide shelter for hibernating beneficial insects, delay pruning established specimens until early spring, when up to a third of the oldest flowering shoots can be cut back to ground level. Afterward, mulch with compost or well-rotted manure around the base.

The bright flowers of coral honeysuckle are particularly alluring to hummingbirds in warm climates.

## Honesty, satin flower

### Zones 5–9

Honesty, an attractive hardy annual or biennial, is popular with pollinating insects and birds. Easily grown from seed sown the previous spring, it forms well-branched plants growing to 36 in. (90 cm) tall, clothed with heart-shaped, midgreen leaves. The clusters of sweetly scented, violet-purple or white flowers that emerge from the leaf axils in late spring and early summer are a good source of nectar for butterflies and bees. If left intact, the translucent, flat, round seedpods that follow adorn the winter garden for months, providing food for hungry finches and ample opportunities for the plant to self-seed.

*L. a.* 'Munstead Purple' is a striking form with dark reddish purple flowers, originally cultivated by the Edwardian garden designer Gertrude Jeykll. *L. a.* var. *albiflora* has pure white flowers, and *L. a.* var. *albiflora* 'Alba Variegata' combines white flowers and handsomely variegated and margined leaves. Both are useful for brightening up a shady area.

### Where to plant

Honesty is perfect for naturalizing in a woodland edge or wild garden. Although it will grow in any well-drained garden soil, in sun or partial shade, to attract butterflies plant it in direct sunlight in generous drifts with other nectar-rich, spring-flowering plants, such as forget-me-not (*Myosotis sylvatica*) and sweet rocket (*Hesperis matronalis*).

### Caring for plants

Resist the urge to cut back the plant immediately after it has flowered, because the seedpods provide winter food for birds as well as shelter for small insects. In early spring use any surplus self-sown seedlings to fill gaps that have appeared in the border.

Honesty leaves are an essential food source for the young caterpillars of the Orange-tip butterfly.

## Ragged robin

### Zones 3–7

Ragged robin is useful for naturalizing in moist but well-drained areas of the garden. Once a common sight in damp meadows across Europe, this graceful wildflower sends up sprays of pale to bright purple-pink, star-shaped flowers with ragged petals in late spring and early summer. The flowers, which are borne on slender, upright stems and are up to 1.5 in. (4 cm) across, are a magnet for beneficial pollinating insects, including many long-tongued bees and butterflies.

*L. flos-cuculi* 'Nana' is a compact form, ideal for a limited space. It sends up clusters of finely cut pink flowers on 2 to 6 in. (5 to 15 cm) stems from small rosettes of gray-green, glossy leaves.

### Where to plant

Ragged robin is best planted in ground that remains moist over summer, especially if it is grown in full sun. It is ideal for naturalizing in a summer wildflower meadow or wild garden with other tall, nectar-rich wildflowers, such as field scabious (*Knautia arvensis*).

### Caring for plants

In a moist wildflower meadow take care that vigorous species like creeping buttercup (*Ranunculus repens*) do not engulf ragged robin. If creeping buttercup threatens to overtake its neighbors, cut back the whole area just as the ragged robin flowers are starting to fade. Although flowering will be delayed, many of the other meadow wildflowers will reappear later in the season.

In parts of Europe *Lychnis flos-cuculi* provides sustenance for the caterpillars of the Campion and Lychnis moths. The caterpillars feed on the developing flowerbuds at night and hide among the foliage by day.

# *Lysichiton americanus*

## Yellow skunk cabbage, Western skunk cabbage

### Zones 6–8

Yellow skunk cabbage creates a dramatic display in moist areas of the garden in early spring, when few other water plants are in bloom. The bright yellow, poker-like flowers emit a musky scent, which is unpleasant for humans but which attracts insect pollinators in search of food. Often exceeding 36 in. (90 cm) in length, the huge, paddle-shaped leaves that unfurl after the flowers offer shelter for amphibians and small water birds. Although yellow skunk cabbage self-seeds freely, it is comparatively slow to mature, and it's not unusual for specimens grown from seed collected in late summer to take six years to flower.

White skunk cabbage (*L. camtschatcensis*) is a smaller, white-flowered form. Perfect for where space is limited, it produces pale green poker-like flowers clothed in pure white spathes. These are followed by lustrous, dark green leaves, also up to 36 in. (90 cm) long.

### Where to plant

Yellow skunk cabbage thrives in deep, moist, humus-rich soil in partial shade. For maximum impact, plant in multiples of three in a bog garden, or along the moist margins of a pond or stream.

### Caring for plants

To provide shelter for amphibians, small water birds and insects, do not remove the faded foliage until early spring. Self-sown seedlings can be removed at the same time and replanted where there is sufficient space for the large leaves to unfurl.

The hooded flowers of yellow skunk cabbage look stunning reflected on the surface of a pond or slow-moving stream.

# *Mahonia aquifolium*

## Oregon grape, holly-leaved barberry

### Zones 5–8

Oregon grape is a valuable low-growing, evergreen shrub for the spring garden. Clusters of slightly fragrant, bright yellow flowers provide nectar for insects emerging from winter hibernation, and birds love the bluish black berries that follow. When it is planted in reliably moist soil, the plant's spiny, holly-like leaflets remain handsome all year, often becoming tinged with bronze or purple in winter.

Cultivars suitable for small spaces include *M. a.* 'Smaragd', which has large flowers and lustrous, emerald-green foliage, and *M. a.* 'Orange Flame', which has handsome orange-bronze foliage, becoming red-tinted in winter. The low-growing *M. repens*, which has matte green leaves that turn purplish in winter, creates a dense carpet about 12 in. (30 cm) above the ground.

### Where to plant

Grow in fertile, moist, well-drained soil, protected from drying winds. Planted singly or in groups, Oregon grape provides excellent groundcover for shady areas of a mixed or shrub border, although it will tolerate sun if the soil remains moist.

### Caring for plants

Cut any diseased sections back to ground level, then water and feed — the plant will soon regenerate. Restrict growth by removing unwanted suckers that emerge toward the edge of the plant in spring after flowering, but retain as many of the berried branches as possible as food for birds.

*Mahonia aquifolium* 'Green Ripple' has lustrous dark-green leaves with gently undulating wavy edges.

# *Malus* species and cultivars

## Crab apple

### Zones 4–8

A flowering crab apple with long-lasting fruit is an ideal tree for a small wildlife-friendly garden. In spring the clouds of white or pink-flushed, cup-shaped flowers that smother the branches are popular with early-flying bees. The glossy, green or reddish purple leaves that follow the blossoms cope well with urban pollution, and in some cases color well before they are shed. But it is in late autumn and early winter that crab apples are at their best. The small, glossy, cherry-like fruit that cling to the leafless branches until early winter are an important food for birds and other wildlife.

Both *M.* 'Prairie Fire', which has dark pinkish red blossom and reddish purple fruit, and *M.* 'Donald Wyman', which has white spring flowers followed by abundant red fruit, are round-headed species with excellent disease resistance. *M.* x *schiedeckeri* 'Red Jade', with white or pink-flushed flowers followed by bright red fruit, is a compact, weeping tree, perfect for a small urban or suburban site. Siberian crabapple (*M. baccata*), which has white flowers followed by red or yellow fruit, is ideal for cold climates since it is reliably hardy to Zone 2.

### Where to plant

Crab apples grow well in most soils, except those that are waterlogged or very dry. An open, sunny site is generally preferable; fruits on trees grown in partial shade are slower to ripen. Crab apples are usually planted as specimen trees, in a border or set in the middle of a lawn.

### Caring for plants

To encourage the development of an open, well-shaped crown, remove any dead, diseased and crossing branches in late winter.

The interwoven branches of a *Malus* 'Evereste' make an excellent nesting site.

# *Matthiola longipetala* subsp. *bicornis* (syn. *Matthiola bicornis*)

## Night-scented stock

### Zones 9–10

Night-scented stocks are one of the best summer-flowering annuals for attracting night-flying pollinators. Easily grown from seed sown outdoors in spring, the plants produce a succession of pale lilac flowers about half an inch (15 mm) across throughout the summer. At dusk and on cloudy days the diminutive flowers emit an intoxicating fragrance that nighttime pollinators, such as the Hawk moth, find hard to resist. In the right position, the plant's delicious sweet scent, sometimes described as a mixture of almond and vanilla, will perfume outdoor seating areas and indoor rooms with windows opening on to the garden.

In addition to the pale lilac form, many seed merchants offer *M. b.* 'Starlight Scentsation', a mixture of pastel pink, pale mauve and purple night-scented flowers on plants growing to 18 in. (45 cm) tall.

### Where to plant

Night-scented stocks like a sunny spot and moderately fertile, moist but well-drained soil. To guarantee a long display, make several sowings from early to late spring in finely raked soil. Press the seeds gently into the soil but do not cover them, because they need light to germinate. To enjoy the scent, choose an open site below a window, close to a house entrance or near a patio.

### Caring for plants

Night-scented stocks are prone to fungal diseases, such as downy mildew and gray mold, but you can minimize the risk of this by following a number of simple steps. Choose an open site where air circulation is good; resist over-sowing the seeds. When the seedlings are large enough to handle, thin to 3 in. (8 cm) apart. Finally, whenever possible water established plants at ground level, rather than from above, to avoid wetting the leaves.

The small four-petaled flowers of night-scented stock have a deliciously sweet scent that is out of all proportion to their size. Because the flowers are closed in daylight it is often recommended they are sown together with Virginian stock (*Malcolmia maritima*), which provides nectar for day-flying pollinators.

# *Mentha aquatica*

## Watermint

### Zones 6–11

In summer the powderpuff-like, lilac flowers of watermint provide nectar for visiting butterflies and bees. This is a fast-growing, groundcover plant for stabilizing the muddy margins of a wildlife pond or stream, where it will create a lush carpet of peppermint-scented, dark green leaves and erect, reddish purple stems, which offer shelter for small amphibians and water bugs. Watermint foliage also provides food for the emerging caterpillars of several European species of moth, including the Water Ermine and Large Ranunculus moth.

The species can be invasive. Compact forms include the highly ornamental *M. a.* var. *crispa*, which has crinkled and curled spearmint-scented leaves, and the narrow-leaved *M. a.* 'Mandeliensis'.

### Where to plant

Grow watermint around the shallow margins of a wildlife pond or slow-moving stream in water that is no deeper than 3 in. (8 cm). To prevent it from overtaking other smaller, less vigorous plants, contain the roots in an aquatic planting basket, topdressed with pea shingle or gravel. To encourage butterflies, site plants in direct sunlight with early-blooming marginals, such as marsh marigold (*Caltha palustris*), which will provide nectar before watermint flowers open.

### Caring for plants

In late summer trim back any stems that are beginning to encroach on smaller, less vigorous plants. Leave prunings next to the pond for several days to allow any small creatures sheltering in the foliage to re-enter the water.

The nectar-rich flowers of watermint encourage butterflies to visit the margins of a wildlife pond.

# *Monarda didyma*

## Bergamot, bee balm, Oswego tea

36in 90cm    18in 45cm

### Zones 4–9

Bergamot is a bushy, aromatic perennial, much loved by beneficial pollinating insects and birds. Planted in soil that remains moist over summer, it will produce whorls of nectar-rich, bright scarlet or pink flowers on square, self-supporting stems over a long period from midsummer to early fall. In addition to providing autumn food for small birds, the seedheads and stiff, vertical stems look attractive when they are rimed with frost in the winter garden.

Many bergamot hybrids, including those named after the signs of the zodiac, have been bred to be resistant to powdery mildew. These include the pale purple-violet *M.* 'Aquarius' and pale pink *M.* 'Fishes'. *M.* 'Marshall's Delight', which has clear pink flowers, is one of the best of the older mildew-resistant hybrids, consistently outperforming more recent introductions in trials.

*Monarda* 'Mohawk' is one of the newer bergamot hybrids that have better resistance to powdery mildew.

Facing page: In warmer zones, these brilliant pink flowers are a magnet for hummingbirds, as well as pollinating insects.

### Where to plant

Grow in fertile, moist but well-drained soil that does not dry out completely in summer. Try to choose a spot where air circulates freely. Plant in small groups in sun or partial shade in a mixed or herbaceous border, kitchen garden or herb garden.

### Caring for plants

To minimize the risk of powdery mildew, mulch with garden compost or well-rotted manure and water regularly during prolonged dry spells. Do not cut back stems until midspring to provide food for seed-eating birds and shelter for overwintering insects. Lift and divide congested colonies every second or third year.

# Nicotiana sylvestris

## Tobacco plant

### Zones 9–11

Ornamental tobacco plants are one of the stars of the night-blooming garden. Usually grown as annuals in all but the warmest zones, they quickly form handsome rosettes of large, dark green, lyre-shaped leaves. The pure white, trumpet-shaped flowers that emerge on tall stems in summer and early fall are the key to the plants' success. As the temperature drops at dusk they start to release a wonderful musky, tuberose-like fragrance, which night-flying insects find particularly alluring. Although the flowers close in bright sunshine, on overcast, dull summer days they will often be visited by day-flying pollinators, such as butterflies and hummingbirds.

*Take care when handling the plants — contact with the foliage may cause skin irritation.*

### Where to plant

Tobacco plants like a warm, sunny spot and fertile, moist but well-drained soil. The large leaves lose a lot of water on hot days, so the plants perform best where they receive some shade from the hot afternoon sun. Typically growing to 5 ft. (1.5 m) tall, they look best planted in groups toward the back of a border, in a semi-wild garden or close to an outdoor seating area.

### Caring for plants

Tobacco plants are seldom troubled by any serious insect damage or disease. To prolong the flowering period remove the spent blooms and water regularly, particularly in dry spells, applying a balanced liquid fertilizer every two weeks.

Tobacco plants can only be pollinated by long-tongued insects such as butterflies, moths and bumblebees, which can access the nectar at the base of the long, tubular flowers.

# *Oenothera* cultivars

## Evening primrose, sundrop

### Zones 4–10

Evening primrose is an important source of nectar for night-flying moths and day-flying insects. Opening at dawn or dusk, the saucer-shaped, yellow, pink or red flowers, each of which lasts for just one day, are borne over a long period in summer on upright or trailing stems clothed with whorls of pointed leaves. One of the stars of the moonlit garden, the short-lived blooms are visited by flower flies, bees and butterflies during the day.

Oenothera cultivars are available in a range of heights and attractive foliage and flower colors. *O. speciosa* 'Siskiyou' is a dainty, low-growing form with pink flowers that open during the day. The midborder form *O. versicolor* 'Sunset Boulevard' has vivid, orange-red flowers and red-ribbed, rich green leaves. The tall, red-stemmed *O. fruticosa* 'Fyrverkeri' has deep yellow flowers and purple-tinted leaves.

### Where to plant

Grow in poor to moderately fertile, well-drained soil. Planted in groups, low-growing forms are ideal for softening hard landscaping, while tall forms provide vertical interest in a sunny border or wildlife garden.

### Caring for plants

Protect emerging foliage from slug and snail damage by using beer traps or eco-friendly pellets. Lift and divide large groups of evening primrose in early spring and mulch generously with compost or well-rotted manure.

Moths and other night-flying pollinators are drawn to evening primrose by its delicate, sweet scent.

## *Origanum*

## Oregano, wild marjoram

**Zones 5–9**

If you are creating a wildlife-friendly herb garden from scratch, oregano is a must-have. Easily grown from root cuttings, this sun-loving, woody perennial produces whorls of tubular, pink-purple or white flowers on upright or spreading stems from midsummer to early fall. The nectar-rich blooms, which remain attractive for many weeks, are a favorite with butterflies and bumblebees. Oregano is also valuable in the vegetable garden, where it can be planted between rows of brassicas so that Cabbage White butterflies will be encouraged to lay their eggs on the undersides of the strongly aromatic, dark green, oval leaves in preference to nearby crops. In winter the plants provide food for many seed-eating birds and shelter for hibernating insects.

There is a wide range of ornamental and culinary varieties of oregano, some available only from specialist herb growers. Ornamental cultivars, such as *O. laevigatum* 'Herrenhausen', which has dense whorls of pink flowers, red-purple stems and purple-flushed young leaves, and *O. l.* 'Hopleys', which produces dainty heads of deep pink flowers, surrounded by purple bracts, and small dark green leaves, have been shown to be more attractive to butterflies than those grown for culinary use. Both *O. vulgare* 'Aureum', which has pink flowers and aromatic, golden-yellow leaves, and the curly leafed *O. v.* 'Aureum Crispum' grow to 12 in. (30 cm) high, making them ideal choices for edging paths and borders.

**Where to plant**

Oregano prefers well-drained, slightly alkaline soil and a position in full sun. However, as the foliage of the golden-leaved forms scorches in intense sunlight, they are best planted where they will be in shade at midday. Seeds are slow

Facing page: *O. vulgare* 'Thumble's Variety' has edible golden variegated leaves and white flowers that attract butterflies.

to germinate, so it is better to start with small plants or root cuttings. To attract butterflies grow several large clumps with other nectar-rich herbs, such as thyme, rosemary and sage.

**Caring for plants**

Although oregano prefers well-drained conditions, it dries out quickly, so remember to water frequently, especially in hot, dry spells. To provide a place for insects to overwinter, do not cut back the flowered stems until early spring.

The leaves of culinary forms of oregano may be used, fresh or dried, for flavoring pizza toppings and stews.

# *Papaver orientale* cultivars

## Oriental poppy

### Zones 2–7

Single-flowered Oriental poppies are easy-to-grow perennials, popular with pollinating insects and birds. From late spring to midsummer, plants produce erect stems topped with large, showy, bright red, crepe-paperlike blooms from clumps of bristly, toothed, midgreen leaves. Pollinators love the open, cup-shaped flowers, which give easy access to the nectar. After flowering, both the stems and the seedheads turn a beautiful muted shade of brown. If they are left in place, the seedheads are a source of interest and a place for small birds to perch while they are feeding on the seeds.

Oriental poppies come in a wide range of colors, from pure white to rich shades of pink, red and deep, rich purple. Some of the newer cultivars, which have upward-facing blooms and sturdy stems, are particularly useful for the wildlife garden. *P. o.* 'Allegro' has bright orange-scarlet flowers, 4 to 6 in. (10 to 15 cm) across, with a distinctive black eye. *P. o.* 'Beauty of Livermere' is an old garden favorite, that bears large, vivid red flowers, to 8 in. (20 cm) across, with black blotches at the base of each petal. *P. o.* 'Black and White', which has pure white flowers, blotched crimson-black at the base, works especially well with plants with silver-gray foliage. The pleated, mulberry-plum petals of the much sought-after *P. o.* 'Patty's Plum' have been compared with the faded silk of antique ballgowns.

### Where to plant

Oriental poppies prefer a sunny spot and well-drained soil. On very fertile ground the plants may produce a lot of topgrowth and require staking. They are best grown toward the middle or back of the border with some late-flowering perennials, such as sunflowers and dahlias, which help to mask the faded foliage that remains once plants have finished flowering.

### Caring for plants

Leave the faded seedheads to provide food for birds and an opportunity for the plant to self-seed. To encourage germination, the surrounding ground should be left uncovered until the following spring when the seedlings start to appear.

Oriental poppies are versatile plants that work equally well in modern gardens and in more relaxed cottage-style borders.

# *Parthenocissus* species and cultivars

## Virginia creeper

**Zones 4–9**

Virginia creeper is a versatile, deciduous vine that provides shelter and food for a range of insects and birds. It is one of the food plants of the Virginia creeper Sphinx Moth: female moths lay eggs on the undersides of the deeply divided, three- or five-lobed leaves, and the inconspicuous, greenish summer flowers provide nectar for the fully grown adults. In addition to providing a spectacular show, the flame-colored fall foliage alerts birds to the plant's fat-packed fruit. Although disagreeable to humans, at least 30 species of birds, including thrushes, woodpeckers, robins and sparrows, find the blue-black berries a tasty and nutritious treat.

It is important to suit the vigor and ultimate size of the plant with the size of the site. Chinese Virginia creeper (*P. henryana*), which has deeply divided, velvety dark green leaves with white and pink veins, is less rampant than some species and is perfect for a limited space. On the other hand, *P. tricuspidata* 'Lowii', which has deeply lobed, dark green leaves with frilled margins turning shades of red and purple in autumn, and *P. quinquefolia*, which has deeply divided, midgreen leaves becoming crimson-red, are extremely vigorous and suitable for a medium to large site only.

### Where to plant

Grow in fertile, well-drained soil in sun or shade. Virginia creeper is ideal for covering a north- or east-facing wall or for growing through a strong tree. Give the vine a good start by incorporating plenty of well-rotted organic matter in the planting hole, and support the young growth with bamboo canes until it can support itself.

### Caring for plants

After leaf-fall avoid clearing away all the fallen leaves — not only do they look attractive on the ground but fully grown caterpillars of the Virginia creeper Sphinx Moth overwinter among the leaves in loosely spun cocoons. Prune established plants in early winter, paying particular attention to any stems that are encroaching on windows, guttering or roofs.

A mature Virginia creeper offers good cover, food and a safe nesting site for a range of birds.

# *Primula veris*

## Cowslip, cowslip primrose

### Zones 3–8

Cowslips are a vital source of nectar for early-flying pollinators. In mid- to late spring, stems bearing nodding clusters of deep yellow flowers emerge from rosettes of midgreen, oblong leaves. The sweet scent of the flowers attracts bees and helps them find the nectar. Cowslips naturally increase by self-seeding, but you can easily help them along by sowing freshly collected seed, gathered toward the end of spring, on the surface of a gritty starter mix. After an initial "chilling" in a refrigerator for about 10 days, the container should be placed outside in a sheltered spot and kept moist until the following spring when a crop of new seedlings will have appeared.

### Where to plant

Although cowslips will generally tolerate most garden soils, they must have a humus-rich, moisture-retentive soil if they are in full sun. For maximum impact, plant in bold groups on a grassy bank, wildflower border or woodland edge, under the dappled shade cast by deciduous shrubs and trees.

### Caring for plants

Where cowslips are naturalized in sections of a lawn or meadow, delay cutting the grass until early summer so that they have time to set seed.

Cowslips that are naturalized in lawns should be planted in an inconspicuous spot where the grass can be left uncut until early summer without looking untidy.

## *Prunus padus*

## Bird cherry, European bird cherry

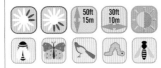

### Zones 3–6

The European bird cherry is a medium-sized, deciduous tree that is popular with a range of wildlife. Mature specimens become rather spreading, but younger trees are usually upright in habit and often have a rounded crown. Various butterfly and moth caterpillars feed on the finely toothed, dark green leaves that unfurl in late spring, and many pollinating insects visit the clusters of almond-scented, cup-shaped white flowers that open soon after the leaves unfurl. The small, shiny black cherries that follow are among the earliest fruit to ripen. Although inedible for humans, they provide a feast for adult songbirds and the energy they need to rear their young. The leaves often turn spectacular shades of red or gold before they are shed, and the dark, reddish brown peeling bark is a handsome winter feature. Taken together, these characteristics make the bird cherry one of the best four-season ornamental trees available to the wildlife-friendly gardener.

Virginian bird cherry (*P. virginia*), which has cup-shaped, white flowers in late spring followed by small red or purple fruits, is a closely related North American species. It is both more compact and more conical in shape than the European bird cherry.

### Where to plant

Although the bird cherry is easily grown in any well-drained soil in full sun or partial shade, the flowers and fall color are superior on trees growing in an open, sunny site. This is an excellent specimen tree for a small or medium-sized garden, casting light shade that allows plants such as spring-flowering bulbs to flourish beneath the canopy.

### Caring for plants

Like most ornamental cherries, the bird cherry requires minimal pruning, which should be carried out while the tree is still young. In early spring remove any dead, diseased or crossing branches, along with any suckers that appear at the base of the tree. Keep pruning wounds as small as possible to minimize the opportunities for the tissue to become infected.

In spring the young leaves of the bird cherry are host to several butterfly and moth caterpillars, including the Small Ermine moth.

# *Pyracantha* cultivars

## Firethorn

### Zones 5–9

Planting one of the newer disease-resistant cultivars of firethorn is a great way to support wildlife. The dense, spiny branches of these hardy evergreen shrubs are good cover for nesting birds and protect them from predators. In late spring and early summer the plants produce clusters of small, white hawthorn-like flowers that are popular with nectar-loving insects. The long-lasting fruits that follow provide important winter food for resident songbirds.

It is worth looking out for cultivars selected for their cold-hardiness and tolerance of disease. *P.* 'Mohave' is a vigorous and free-flowering form producing masses of long-lasting red berries, and *P.* 'Saphyr Orange' is a vigorous variety with persistent fruits maturing to orange; both offer good resistance to cold weather, scab and fireblight.

*The seeds of firethorn may cause a mild stomach upset if eaten.*

### Where to plant

Firethorns require fertile, well-drained soil and a position in sun or partial shade. They also need plenty of space in which to spread. They can be grown as freestanding shrubs, fan-trained against a wall or in an informal flowering hedge. To minimize frost damage to the foliage choose a sheltered, partly shaded site in cold climates.

### Caring for plants

Wall-trained specimens should be pruned in mid- or late summer, shortly after they have flowered, to reveal the ripening berries. Remember to wear stout gardening gloves and goggles as protection against the sharp thorns.

Firethorns are a good choice for attracting wildlife to city gardens because they cope well with urban pollution and with poor and compacted soils.

# Rhamnus frangula (syn. *Frangula alnus*)

## Alder buckthorn, glossy buckthorn

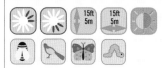

**Zones 3–7**

Alder buckthorn is ideal for creating a wildlife-friendly hedge or screen. Relatively fast-growing, this large, deciduous shrub has a network of upright and spreading branches among which birds love to nest. The glossy, oval, dark green leaves, which turn red before they are shed in fall, provide birds with good cover against predators. In late spring and early summer butterflies and bees are attracted to the clusters of tiny, whitish green flowers, and many birds enjoy the black autumn fruits. In Europe the main reason for growing this shrub is that it is one of only two food plants of the caterpillars of the Brimstone butterfly. In late spring the female lays eggs singly on the underside of a fresh leaf, usually on the sunniest side of the bush.

Tallhedge glossy buckthorn (*R. f.* 'Columnaris') is a strongly upright form, often offered by specialist nurseries for hedging. *R. f.* 'Aspleniifolia' has narrow leaves with distinctive wavy margins, which give the plant an overall fern-like texture.

In the Northeast and prairie areas of North America both the species and these two cultivars are considered potentially invasive. If you garden in these regions plant a noninvasive native shrub, such as American cranberrybush (*Viburnum trilobum* syn. *V. opulus* var. *americanum*) instead.

*All parts of the plant may cause severe discomfort if eaten.*

### Where to plant

Alder buckthorn grows best in moist, moderately fertile soil, in sun or partial shade. In addition to its wildlife-attracting properties, it can be grown singly in a shrub or mixed border or used to make a screen for garbage bins or compost piles.

### Caring for plants

If you are growing alder buckthorn as a food plant for the Brimstone butterfly, prune the tips of the branches after planting to encourage more fresh, young shoots. To prevent large numbers of caterpillars from defoliating a single specimen in late spring, carefully pick off some of them as soon as they appear and put them on the leaves of another nearby host plant.

*Note: Listed as an invasive plant in Minnesota.*

*Rhamnus frangula* 'Aspleniifolia' is commonly offered by nurseries specializing in hedging plants.

# *Ribes odoratum* (syn. *Ribes aureum*)

## Buffalo currant, golden currant

### Zones 5–9

Buffalo currant is one of the best spring-flowering shrubs for wildlife, providing an early source of nectar for pollinating insects and good nesting cover and food for birds. It spreads by suckers to form thickets of arching stems, which are clothed in bright green, lobed leaves that turn magenta, sulfur-yellow and purple in fall. In early and midspring the plant produces drooping clusters of fragrant, golden-yellow flowers, which fill the air with a deliciously spicy, clove-like scent, particularly alluring to early-flying butterflies. The red or purplish black pea-sized fruits that follow in summer can be made into pies or jam, but the wildlife-friendly gardener will leave them to be foraged by songbirds and small mammals.

The flowers of the buffalo currant are attractive not only to butterflies and bees but also to the ruby-throated hummingbird, and it is one of the key plants in flower along the northerly migration route that the birds take in spring.

### Where to plant

Although buffalo currant prefers moderately well-drained soil, the plant appears to cope well in poor soils. It is suitable for growing as a single specimen in a sunny shrub border or in groups along the margins of a woodland garden. The open, arching form allows it to be successfully underplanted with a carpet of shade-tolerant, spring-flowering plants, such as sweet rocket (*Hesperis matronalis*) or masterwort (*Astrantia alba* subsp. *involucratae*).

### Caring for plants

Left unpruned, buffalo currant spreads by suckering to form dense thickets of unproductive wood. To promote fresh, new growth, superior flowers and fruit, prune established specimens every year immediately after flowering, removing one-quarter to one-third of the oldest branches to ground level.

## *Rosa* species and cultivars

# Rose

### Zones 3–9

Planting one of the older, hip-bearing species roses or one of the closely descended modern hybrids will help to encourage birds to take up residence. Grown as an informal, flowering hedge, the stems and semi-evergreen foliage provide a safe nesting site, away from predators. In early and midsummer the open, cup-shaped flowers are popular with insect pollinators. In late summer and early autumn the hips develop against a backdrop of fiery foliage. These often persist until late winter in mild conditions and are an important food source for birds. Disease resistant and winter hardy, it is especially suitable for gardens in cold climates.

   *R. glauca*, which bears small, cerise-pink flowers on almost thornless stems and spherical, red hips, is primarily grown for its delicate leaves, which have an ethereal, grayish purple sheen. An extremely vigorous rose, it produces the best foliage when the stems are cut back to ground level every second year. *R.* 'Geranium'

has scented, single cherry-red flowers with a creamy center, an attractive arching habit and distinctive, flagon-shaped, bright scarlet hips.

### Where to plant

Species roses may be grown as a single specimen or as an informal, flowering hedge. Although all roses perform best in full sun, they are surprisingly tolerant of partial shade, poor soil and exposed, windy sites.

### Caring for plants

Species roses show excellent resistance to pests and diseases that affect many modern hybrids. To minimize the impact on wildlife, delay pruning until late winter, when birds will have stripped most or all of the fruits from the plant.

When birds have other sources of food and conditions are mild, the orange-red hips of the hardy *Rosa rugosa* often remain intact until late winter.

# *Rosmarinus officinalis* cultivars

## Rosemary

### Zones 8–10

Rosemary is one of the most useful aromatic herbs for luring pollinating insects and birds into a garden. Given a sheltered sunny site, this shrubby evergreen plant often produces a first flush of tubular, purple-blue, pink or white flowers in early spring, when there are few other sources of nectar around. The tiny flowers, borne at the axils of the dark green, needle-like leaves, appear again intermittently in summer and autumn, although in smaller numbers. As well as pollinators, rosemary also benefits many birds that forage for the insects that shelter in its dense foliage, such as aphids.

Specialist nurseries and herb farms offer a wide range of cultivars with purple-blue, pink and white flowers and with upright or creeping habits. *R. o.* 'Majorca Pink', which has pale lavender-pink flowers, is a compact form with a unique upward growth habit. Growing to 40 in. (about 1 m) tall and wide, the flowers are borne on narrow, tufted shoots that lean out from the center of the plant and curve up at the tip. *R. o.* 'Miss Jessopp's Upright' (syn. *R. o.* 'Fastigiatus'), which has blue speckled flowers, is a vigorous, upright form with a distinctive multistemmed habit that grows to 6 ft. (1.8 m) tall. Plants in the *R. o.* Prostratus Group are ground hugging and rarely exceed 24 in. (60 cm) tall, with sparsely branched foliage and mid- to pale blue speckled flowers.

### Where to plant

Like other natives of countries around the Mediterranean, rosemary needs free-drained soil and full sun. Amend clay soils with coarse horticultural sand. While the strongly upright cultivars are useful for providing vertical interest in a sunny border or herb garden, the low-growing forms look great cascading over the edges of an old stone wall or raised bed.

### Caring for plants

Rosemary should be pruned immediately after it has flowered in spring to encourage fresh, young growth. The prunings can be put to good use on the first barbecue of the year to enhance the flavor of roasted vegetables, lamb and pork.

Strongly upright cultivars, such as *Rosmarinus officinalis* 'Miss Jessopp's Upright', may be used to create a flowering aromatic hedge.

# *Rudbeckia* species and cultivars

## Black-eyed Susan, coneflower

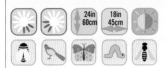

### Zones 3–10

Black-eyed Susans are an important late source of nectar for insects and seeds for overwintering birds. These plants are easily grown from seed, sometimes flowering in the same year. From late summer until the first frosts they produce a succession of golden-orange or yellow daisy-like flowers, with cone-shaped, blackish brown centers, from clumps of hairy, midgreen leaves. Ultraviolet markings on the petals attract and guide insects to the center of the flower.

*R. fulgida* var. *deamii* is a particularly free-flowering variety with orange-yellow flowers 3 in. (8 cm) across, while *R. f.* var. *sullivantii* 'Goldsturm' produces large, golden-yellow flowers 5 in. (13 cm) across. At 24 in. (60 cm) tall, both are considerably shorter than the species. *R. hirta* 'Becky Mixed' is a low-growing form, with lemon-yellow to bright orange flowers 6 in. (15 cm) across on 10 in. (25 cm) stems. Neat and compact, it is ideal for filling gaps in a border, or for use in containers.

### Where to plant

Black-eyed Susans will grow in any well-drained soil in full sun or partial shade. Although relatively drought-tolerant once established, the plants appreciate regular watering and a site that does not dry out completely over summer. They look best when they are grown in generous drifts with other late summer-flowering perennials and ornamental grasses.

### Caring for plants

Throughout summer water and deadhead regularly to prolong flowering. To provide food for seed-eating birds delay cutting back the faded flowerheads until the following spring, when any unwanted self-sown seedlings can also be removed.

This black-eyed Susan has ultraviolet markings on its petals. Invisible to humans, they guide pollinating insects like this bee to the center of the flower.

# *Salvia* cultivars

## Sage

### Zones 4–9

As well as adding a splash of color to summer borders, salvias provide a valuable late source of nectar when other flowers are finished. Easily grown in most garden soils, these hardy perennials send up dense spires of two-lipped, rich purple, violet-blue or pink flowers above clumps of wrinkled, gray-green leaves in early and midsummer. As long as the faded flower spires are removed promptly the plants will often flower again in early autumn. For butterflies and bees this second flush of nectar-rich blooms appears just when they need to build up reserves of energy to survive through winter, or migrate to warmer climes.

Many of the cultivars offered for sale by garden centers and plant nurseries are selections of wood sage (*Salvia nemorosa*) or the hybrid *Salvia* x *sylvestris*. *S. n.* 'Ostfriesland' (syn. 'East Friesland'), which has rich purple-blue flowers, and *S. n.* 'Wesuwe', which has violet-purple flowers with dark reddish bracts, are compact forms of wood sage, invaluable for small spaces. *S.* x *s.* 'Mainacht' (syn. 'May Night') begins to flower in late spring, producing a succession of large, indigo-blue flowers, to 0.75 in. (2 cm) long, until midsummer. *S.* x *s.* 'Rose Queen' has bright rose-pink flowers, opening from dark pink buds. Flowering in the first year from seed sown earlier in the season, it is perfect for gardeners on a budget.

### Where to plant

Salvias flourish in most moderately fertile, moist but well-drained soils. Drought-tolerant once established, they are a good choice for a gravel garden or for filling gaps in the border left by spring-flowering perennials and bulbs. Salvias look best when they are planted in groups in a warm sunny spot, particularly if you want to attract butterflies.

Facing page: *S.* x *s.* 'Mainacht' develops beautiful indigo-blue flowers that last until midsummer.

### Caring for plants

Cut back the flower spires promptly as soon as they start to fade to encourage a second flush. Then, to provide shelter for overwintering insects, do not cut back the second flush of flowers until early spring, when large clumps can also be divided.

From midsummer to fall, salvias such as this vibrant *Salvia nemorosa* 'Ostfriesland', are a magnet for butterflies and bees. Butterflies prefer to visit stands of flowers, so avoid growing plants as single specimens.

# *Sambucus* cultivars

## Elder

**Zones 3–9**

Planting an ornamental elder is a great way of providing wildlife with shelter and food. Although these multistemmed, deciduous shrubs can attain tree-like dimensions, they are usually kept compact by annual pruning. In early or midsummer the branches are smothered with flattened heads of small, creamy white flowers, which are a good source of nectar for pollinating insects. The clusters of glossy black or red berries that develop at the tips of the branches are edible if cooked, but in late autumn and early winter they are food for many songbirds and small mammals. Birds sometimes gorge themselves on the overripe fruit, becoming mildly intoxicated on the fermented juice.

   *S. canadensis* 'Laciniata', which has white flowers in midsummer followed by maroon-black fruits, is a cut-leaf form of the American elderberry. *S. c.* 'Maxima' has extra-large leaves and enormous flowerheads, to 18 in. (45 cm) across, but despite the size of the foliage and flowers it seldom grows taller than 10 ft. (3 m). *S. nigra* 'Aurea' is a golden-leaved form of the European elderberry (Zones 5–8); it has musk-scented white flowers in early summer followed by black fruits. *S. n.* 'Black Beauty' has intense, black-burgundy foliage and lemon-scented, pale pink flowers, opening from dark red buds. *S. racemosa* 'Plumosa Aurea' and *S. r.* 'Sutherland Gold' are popular cultivars of the red-berried elder (Zones 3–7). Both have creamy yellow flowers in midspring, followed by red fruits and deeply cut, bronze young leaves, which turn golden-yellow as they mature.

*All parts of the plant may cause severe discomfort if eaten, and contact with the leaves may cause skin irritation.*

### Where to plant

Elders prefer moist, well-drained, humus-rich soil, but they will tolerate a range of conditions and a position in sun or partial shade. Use singly in a shrub or mixed border or in groups to create a wildlife-friendly hedge or screen.

### Caring for plants

For the best effect elders should be cut back to ground level each year in early spring. Although this may seem drastic, regular annual pruning helps to keep the plant at a manageable size and promote the growth of additional and larger leaves.

*Sambucus racemosa* 'Sutherland Gold' is less susceptible to sun-scorch than other golden cut-leaved varieties. Like all yellow-leafed forms it is best planted in partial shade, because the delicate young foliage can scorch in full sun.

# *Scabiosa* cultivars

## Pincushion flower, scabious

### Zones 4–8

Pincushion flowers are among the best perennials for attracting butterflies and bees. If they are deadheaded regularly, these versatile, long-blooming plants produce a succession of often sweetly scented, pincushion-like flowerheads on slender wiry stems, above mounds of finely divided, gray-green leaves. Each of the heads actually contains numerous, tiny, nectar-rich flowers, arranged like a small pincushion, that provide butterflies and bees with an almost continuous source of food from late spring until the first frosts.

    *S. atropurpurea* 'Chile Black' is an eye-catching, almost-black cultivar that works equally well in a modern or cottage-style planting scheme. The sweetly scented, deep claret-purple flowerheads are borne on stems 24 in. (60 cm) tall. *S.* 'Butterfly Blue', with lavender-blue flowerheads, and *S.* 'Pink Mist', with deep mauve-pink flowerheads and pale centers, are compact forms, growing to 16 in. (40 cm) wide and tall. The *S. caucasica* Perfecta Series has lavender-blue flowerheads on stems to 24 in. (60 cm) high. At up to 3 in. (8 cm) across, the frilly petalled flowers are larger and showier than those of many other varieties.

### Where to plant

Pincushion flowers thrive in well-drained, neutral to slightly alkaline soil in a full-sun position. Choose a site that will not become waterlogged. They are ideal for a butterfly or wild garden, where they should be planted in bold drifts.

### Caring for plants

Pincushion flowers are untroubled by any major pest or disease, but they tend to be short-lived and should be replaced every three to four years. In summer and autumn, water and deadhead regularly to prolong flowering. Mulching around the base of the plants will help to conserve moisture in long, hot spells.

*Scabiosa caucasica* 'Miss Willmott' produces a succession of greenish-white flowers on 28 in. (70 cm) stems.

# *Sedum* cultivars

## Stonecrop, ice plant

### Zones 3–8

Stonecrops are one of the best perennials for encouraging butterflies and bees. From midsummer the succulent, gray-green, upright stems are topped with flat heads of tiny, star-shaped, pink, pink-mauve or white flowers, offering a valuable late source of nectar for overwintering insects. Maturing to a deep coppery-red, the seedheads provide structure and interest over winter, often staying intact until spring.

Stonecrops are available in a wide range of habit of growth, size, and foliage and flower color. *S. spectabile* 'Brilliant' has bright pinkish mauve flowers, the trailing *S.* 'Ruby Glow' has greenish purple leaves and wine-red flowers, and the tall, upright *S. telephium* 'Matrona' has beet-red-stained stems and pale to dark rose-pink flowers.

### Where to plant

Grow stonecrops in fertile, well-drained soil, neutral to slightly alkaline, and preferably in full sun. Planted singly or in bold drifts toward the front of the border, the robust stems contrast well with the silky flowerheads of the small, airy grass *Stipa tenuissima*.

### Caring for plants

Stonecrops are generally trouble-free. To provide winter cover for insects, do not remove the faded flowerheads until late winter or early spring, then mulch with well-rotted manure or garden compost just before plants start into growth. So that plants do not develop empty centers and to maximize flowering, divide congested clumps every three or four years in spring.

Facing page: *Sedum spectabile* 'Brilliant' is one of the cultivars favored by butterflies and bees.

The flowerheads of *Sedum telephium* 'Matrona' are smaller and more loosely arranged than those of other varieties of stonecrop.

# *Solidago* cultivars

## Golden rod, Aaron's rod

### Zones 3–8

Just when many summer-flowering perennials are coming to a close, the bushy, upright stems of golden rod are crowned with plumes of bright golden-yellow flowers, which are an important source of nectar for many beneficial pollinating insects. Left intact, the seedheads are a favorite autumn food of small birds.

Unless you have a large garden, avoid the species, most of which are potentially invasive and, left unchecked, will quickly colonize a small garden. Several more controllable cultivars have been developed, and among the best compact forms are S. 'Goldenmosa', which has bright yellow mimosa-like flowers on yellow stalks, S. 'Goldkind', which has golden-yellow plumes, and S. 'Cloth of Gold', which has acid-yellow flowers.

### Where to plant

Golden rod does best in sandy, well-drained, poor to moderately fertile soil. Use singly or in small groups in the middle of a sunny border with black-eyed Susans (*Rudbeckia*), coneflowers (*Echinacea*), lanceleaf coreopsis and asters.

### Caring for plants

Support tall-growing forms with brushwood before the flowers appear. Leave ripening seedheads in place until the following year to provide food for birds. In early spring cut back the dead stems, remove any unwanted self-sown seedlings and mulch with well-rotted manure or garden compost.

*Solidago* 'Cloth of Gold' is a compact form, especially suitable for the front of a sunny border.

# *Sorbus* species and cultivars

## Mountain ash

**Zones 3–8**

The mountain ash is one of the best wildlife-friendly species of tree for a small garden. Rarely growing more than 40 ft. (12 m) high, even when fully mature, the trees provide food and shelter for many beneficial insects and songbirds. In early spring, as they unfurl, the handsomely toothed, mid- or deep green leaflets offer sustenance for the caterpillars of several common species of butterfly. From late spring to early summer the heavily scented heads of white, creamy white or pale pink flowers that adorn the tree attract nectar-loving insects. In fall the foliage turns brilliant shades of orange, red or purple — a signal to the resident songbirds that the orange, red or yellow berries that follow the flowers are ripe and ready to eat.

American mountain ash (*Sorbus americana*) forms a rounded to broadly spreading tree with white flowers followed by orange-red berries. The orange-red fruits of European mountain ash (*S. aucuparia*) start to ripen in late summer and are one of the first to be eaten by birds. By comparison, the broadly upright *S.* 'Joseph Rock' holds on to its fruit much longer. Although birds are drawn to the amber-colored berries, they tend to leave them on the tree until other sources of food have been exhausted.

*The fruits may cause a mild stomach upset if eaten by humans.*

**Where to plant**

The trees should be planted in sun or light dappled shade, and thrive in fertile, well-drained, neutral to acidic soils. Versatile and tolerant of pollution, they can be grown as single specimens, in small groups at the edge of a woodland garden or as a wildlife-friendly hedge.

**Caring for plants**

*Sorbus* are prone to fireblight, a potentially fatal bacterial disease, which is first seen when the leaves turn black. Cut back affected branches to at least 24 in. (60 cm) below any signs of the disease and disinfect all pruning tools after use. Established specimens require little pruning, but if necessary, dead or damaged branches should be removed in summer.

The long-lasting fruits of *S.* 'Joseph Rock' are a good source of food for songbirds.

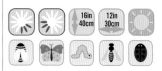

# *Tagetes patula*
## French marigold

### Zones 1–11

French marigolds are one of the most effective companion plants that the organic gardener can grow. The delicate, fern-like leaves emit a powerful aroma that helps to reduce caterpillar damage to brassica crops and to discourage whiteflies in the greenhouse. From early summer to early autumn the rich golden-yellow flowers are visited by many of the "good bugs" that keep insect pests at bay. In addition, secretions from the roots can help to repel nematodes in the soil and to suppress ground elder and couch grass so that gardeners do not have to resort to noxious chemical sprays.

Old-fashioned varieties should be chosen for use as companion plants because the newer forms generally have a less powerful scent. Mexican marigold (*T. minuta*) and African marigold (*T. erecta*) are also useful, although they are taller and require more space.

*Contact with the foliage of all types of French marigold may aggravate skin allergies.*

### Where to plant

French marigolds are easily grown from seed, and do best in a sunny, well-drained site. To minimize caterpillar damage, French marigolds and green vegetable crops need to be started indoors and planted out together in rows.

### Caring for plants

These hardy annuals cope well with both heat and drought, which helps to explain their enduring appeal. Try not to overwater, which encourages fewer flowers and leggy plants, and deadhead regularly to prolong flowering.

French marigolds form compact, bushy plants, which are ideal for growing between green vegetable crops.

# *Thuja plicata* and cultivars

## Western red cedar

### Zones 5–8

Western red cedar provides birds with excellent cover from predators, a nesting site in spring and a warm place to shelter in winter. Many birds and mammals, including squirrels, devour the small, elongated cones that grow among the flattened sprays of mid- or dark green leaves. This majestic evergreen conifer can reach 120 ft. (35 m) tall when fully mature. There are, however, a number of small, less vigorous cultivars, which can be grown as specimen trees or used for hedging, if space is limited.

*T. p.* 'Atrovirens' eventually develops into a tall columnar to conical tree, 120 x 30 ft. (35 x 10 m). *T. p.* 'Hilleri' is a dwarf form with blue-green foliage, which grows to 10 ft. (3 m) tall and wide. *T. p.* 'Zebrina' is a broadly conical tree, 50 x 12 ft. (15 x 4 m) when mature, with yellow-striped, midgreen leaves and small, elliptic cones. Plant it in groups to make an attractive variegated screen or hedge.

*Contact with the foliage may aggravate skin allergies.*

### Where to plant

Western red cedar prefers deep, moist, well-drained soil positioned in full sun, although it will tolerate some shade. It is important to find a site that is sheltered from cold, drying winds.

### Caring for plants

Trim plants grown as hedging in late spring or early summer to minimize any disruption to nesting birds and insects sheltering in the bark. Take care not to cut into the older wood, which will not reshoot, and mulch with well-rotted manure or compost after pruning.

Where *Thuja plicata* 'Atrovirens' is grown as hedging, the dark green foliage forms an excellent backdrop for shrub and herbaceous borders.

# *Thymus* species and cultivars

## Thyme

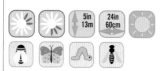

### Zones 5–9

Planting a sun-drenched area of the garden with one of the many attractive creeping thymes is a great way of luring beneficial pollinating insects. As well as releasing a lovely aromatic scent when they are crushed by passing feet, these low-growing herbs produce masses of tiny, nectar-rich flowers in spring and summer, which are highly attractive to butterflies and bees. In large or medium-sized gardens early-mid- and late-blooming cultivars can be combined to create a long-flowering tapestry of contrasting foliage and flowers, which will provide a constant supply of nectar over a long period.

*Thymus polytrichus* subsp. *britannicus* (syn. *T. praecox* subsp. *arcticus*) forms a low carpet of dark green leaves, above which pale to deep purple flowers appear in early and midsummer. Only 2 in. (5 cm) high, it is ideal for planting in the crevices between paving stones. The variegated *T.* 'Doone Valley' grows to 5 in. (13 cm) high. It has lavender-pink flowers in late summer, opening from crimson-red buds, and lemon-scented, dark olive-green leaves with yellow spots. In early and midsummer mother-of-thyme (*T. serpyllum*) produces a sea of small purple-red flowers, borne in tight whorls; it grows to 10 in. (25 cm) high. More suitable for large expanses of ground are mound-forming cultivars such as *T. vulgaris* 'Silver Posie', which has bright purple flowers in late spring and early summer and white-margined, gray-green leaves, and *T.* 'Porlock', which has purple-pink flowers from late spring to midsummer and dark green leaves.

### Where to plant

Thymes thrive in well-drained, neutral to alkaline soil in full sun. Their preference for alkaline conditions makes them perfect for growing in between paving stones or in a border that has recently been cleared of builders' rubble. After planting, topdress with horticultural sand to protect the crown of the plant from becoming waterlogged in winter.

### Caring for plants

Left unpruned, thyme has a tendency to become straggly and woody. To maintain a compact, neat shape, use garden shears to remove a third of the topgrowth immediately after the plant has flowered.

Grow creeping thyme in shallow terracotta pots, placed close to a pathway or entrance, so that you can enjoy the aromatic scent when you brush past.

# *Trachelospermum jasminoides*

## Star jasmine, confederate jasmine

### Zones 8–10

Star jasmine is a wonderfully fragrant, summer-flowering vine, that looks handsome even when not in flower. Initially slow growing, it eventually forms a mass of slender, twining stems, which obediently climb up a wall or scramble over a stout support, such as a pergola. The glossy, dark green oval leaves that cover the stems are retained all year, becoming tinged with bronze or red in winter. From late spring the plant produces clusters of small, pure white, star-shaped flowers intermittently through summer. Moths and other night-flying pollinators are drawn by the luminosity of the flowers and their spicy, jasmine-like fragrance, which intensifies after dusk.

Variegated star jasmine (*T. j.* 'Variegatum') has white-margined and -splashed, gray-green leaves and pure white, jasmine-scented flowers. It is less vigorous and hardy than the plain green form, reaching three-quarters of its height and spread. Glossy star jasmine (*T. j.* 'Wilsonii') has fragrant white flowers that age to cream. The leaves are darker and narrower than the species and turn attractive shades of crimson in the winter months.

### Where to plant

Star jasmine is easily grown in any reasonably fertile, well-drained soil. It is ideal for planting in a sheltered sunny or partially shaded site, where it can be used for covering a fence or wall or trained up a robust tree. It can also be grown in a large container.

### Caring for plants

To prolong flowering, water generously throughout the growing season, applying a liquid fertilizer each month. Delay pruning to early spring to minimize disruption to hibernating insects. Then remove any weak or congested shoots along with the tips of stems that have outgrown their allotted space.

Star jasmine is one of the best vines to plant if you are designing a moonlit garden.

## Tropaeolum majus

## Nasturtium, Indian cress

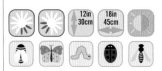

### Zones 4–11

Nasturtiums are one of the best plants that the organic gardener can grow to help reduce colonies of insect pests. From midsummer until the first frosts they produce a succession of funnel-shaped flowers, 1 to 2 in. (2.5 to 5 cm) in diameter, held above mounds of round or kidney-shaped leaves. In addition to butterflies and bees, the flowers are visited by three of the most efficient aphid-feeding insects known to the organic gardener — flower flies, ladybugs and parasitic mini-wasps. Nasturtiums are often grown in the vegetable plot as a sacrifice crop. Not only will they lure aphids away from more valuable edible crops, but they also help to prevent Cabbage White butterflies from laying their eggs on nearby brassicas. This method of planting works because nasturtium leaves have a similar chemical composition and contain mustard oil, to which the butterflies are instinctively drawn.

Cultivated varieties of nasturtium are of two main types, climbers and dwarf, bushy types. The plants in *T. m.* Alaska Series, which grow to about 12 to 18 in. (30 to 45 cm), bear yellow, orange, mahogany, scarlet or cream-colored single flowers. The white-marbled and speckled foliage is guaranteed to create an eye-catching display. In warm zones hummingbirds are drawn to the rich scarlet flowers of *T. m.* 'Empress of India', an heirloom variety named after Queen Victoria, which bears handsome, purple-green leaves and showy, semidouble flowers that are held in high esteem among gardeners. The plants in *T. m.* Tom Thumb Series, which bear yellow, tangerine, red, salmon-pink or rose-pink single flowers, are, at about 10 in. (25 cm) high, among the most compact selections. *T.* Gleam Series produces scarlet, tangerine and yellow semidouble flowers on vigorous, semitrailing stems, which can reach 24 in. (60 cm) or more long.

### Where to plant

Nasturtiums are easily grown from seed, sown outdoors in spring in Zones 4–8 or in winter in Zones 9–11. They perform best in poor, well-drained sandy soils in direct sun or partial shade. In rich, fertile soil nasturtiums tend to produce lots of lush foliage, but few flowers. The dwarf, bushy cultivars are ideal for containers, and climbing or trailing forms are useful for training over a low support or for including in a hanging basket.

### Caring for plants

To prolong flowering water freely and deadhead regularly to remove all spent blooms.

*Tropaeolum majus* 'Tip Top Velvet' is a dwarf variety that is ideal for use in containers.

# Vaccinium corymbosum

## High-bush blueberry

### Zones 5–7

High-bush blueberries are ideal if you garden on moist, very acidic soil and want to attract pollinating insects and birds. They are generally undemanding deciduous shrubs, with narrow, oval or lance-shaped leaves that turn spectacular shades of flame-red and golden-yellow in fall. In late spring and early summer the clusters of urn-shaped, white or pink-tinged flowers that appear at the tips of the branches are an important source of nectar for butterflies and bees. Birds will quickly devour the deliciously sweet, blue-black fruits that follow as soon as they start to turn blue, so if you want to harvest some of the crop for making blueberry muffins or jam, remember to cover the plants securely with 0.75 in. (2 cm) mesh net well before the fruits ripen.

Specialist fruit nurseries offer a range of early, midseason and late cultivars. *V. c.* 'Patriot' produces a heavy crop of large fruit from early to midseason. The midseason *V. c.* 'Bluecrop' is the most widely planted blueberry worldwide, producing a heavy crop of large, flavorsome berries. *V. c.* 'Coville' is a late-fruiting variety with a strongly upright habit.

### Where to plant

High-bush blueberries must have moisture-retentive, acidic soil and a sunny spot. Although self-fertile, fruiting is superior when two or more cultivars are grown next to each other. When you are planting make sure that the roots are just below the surface of the soil and mulch with well-rotted leaf mold or peat moss.

### Caring for plants

Water with rainwater collected in a water barrel and keep well-mulched. To minimize disturbance to any hibernating insects, delay pruning until early spring, when dead, diseased or unproductive branches should be removed to the base of the plant to encourage younger, more productive growth.

Blueberries provide a summer feast for dozens of species of game and songbirds, including robins, grouse, woodpeckers, blue jays and thrushes. Blueberry leaves provide food for caterpillars of the Spring Azure, Brown Elfin and Striped Hairstreak butterflies.

# Verbascum

## Mullein

**Zones 5–8**

Many mulleins are prolific self-seeders, a characteristic that makes them particularly suitable for naturalizing. In the first year the plant concentrates on producing wide rosettes of huge, silver-felted or midgreen leaves. These provide attractive groundcover, food for the caterpillars of the Mullein moth and nesting material for several species of bees. Scores of pollinating insects are drawn to the tall spikes of butter-yellow or white flowers that emerge the following summer. Left intact, the dried flowerheads stand up well through autumn and winter, attracting goldfinches and numerous other small birds.

*V. olympicum* is one of the tallest mulleins, its candelabra-like spires of golden-yellow flowers often exceeding 6 ft. (1.8 m) when fully grown. Where space in the wildlife garden is limited, *V. nigrum*, which has dark yellow flowers, or *V. lychnitis*, which has white flowers with tiny red eyes, are useful alternatives.

In recent years *V.* 'Helen Johnson', with neat, 36 in. (90 cm) spires of purple-eyed, brownish pink flowers, has become one of the most popular garden cultivars. But for long flowering and reliability it is hard to beat *V. chaixii*, which bears spires of maroon-eyed pale yellow flowers, and the white form, *V. c.* 'Album'.

### Where to plant

Mulleins grow best in poor, well-drained, alkaline soil in direct sun. Make sure that you leave sufficient space for the large leaves to develop, because the plant dislikes having to compete for space and light. The tall mulleins make striking focal points in a gravel or wild garden, but the shorter garden varieties are most successful when they are planted in small groups in a cottage-style or mixed border.

### Caring for plants

Left unchecked, Mullein moth caterpillars can quickly defoliate a plant. Minimize damage by picking off the insects as soon as they appear in late spring and early summer and placing them on the leaves of another, less conspicuous specimen. Although some mulleins are strong enough to stand upright, the tall species and garden hybrids need staking in spring, particularly if they are planted in an exposed, windy site.

Moths and other pollinating insects are drawn to the tall spikes of mullein's butter-yellow flowers.

# *Verbena bonariensis*

## Purpletop vervain

### Zones 7–10

It's easy to understand why many butterfly gardeners list purpletop vervain as one of their top 10 plants. With a long flowering period, from early summer until the first frosts, the tightly packed clusters of lilac-purple flowers serve as late "butterfly bars," providing a valuable source of nectar when many native wildflowers are long gone.

In addition to its wildlife credentials, purpletop vervain plays an important role in garden design. The plant's open, transparent shape means that it can easily be used at the front or center of the border because the slender, branching stems will not obscure specimens that are planted behind.

### Where to plant

Grow in moderately fertile, moist but well-drained soil in a sheltered, sunny site. Use in bold drifts to encourage butterflies, or plant throughout the border in small groups to bring cohesion to a planting scheme.

### Caring for plants

When it is grown in partial shade, the plant's tall stems may need to be supported. If this is necessary, use natural materials such as brushwood or twiggy pea-sticks. Protect specimens grown in frost-prone areas with a deep, dry winter mulch around the crown of the plant. To provide shelter for overwintering insects, delay cutting back the faded foliage and seedheads until spring.

Purpletop vervain is a prolific self-seeder, and seedlings often emerge in the most inhospitable places, including between paving stones.

# *Viburnum* species and cultivars

## Viburnum

### Zones 2–8

Planting one of the deciduous forms of viburnum is a great way of providing wildlife with shelter and food for many months of the year. A dense network of branches, covered with dark green, lobed or toothed leaves, provides good cover for songbirds, especially when the shrubs are grouped. In late spring and early summer the plants produce flattened clusters of fragrant, white flowers, which are popular with butterflies and bees. The bright red or blue-black fruits that develop after the flowers often persist well through the winter months, providing an important source of food for birds and other wildlife.

Sheepberry (*V. lentago*), Zones 2–7, is a large, upright shrub or small tree, to 12 ft. (4 m) high and 10 ft. (3 m) wide, with red-purple fall foliage. Many species of birds, including the eastern bluebird, american robin and purple finch, consume its blue-black fruits. *V. opulus* 'Compactum' (Zones 3–8) is a compact, slow-growing form of the European guelder rose, 5 ft. (1.5 m) tall and wide. It has attractive, maple-like leaves, which turn red in fall, and long-lasting, bright red fruits. American cranberrybush (*V. trilobum* syn. *V. o.* var. *americanum*), Zones 2–7, forms a dense, rounded bush 15 x 12 ft. (5 x 4 m). The bright red fruits persist through winter, providing food for some of the earliest spring migrants. *V. plicatum* f. *tomentosum* 'Shasta' (Zones 5–8) produces showy 6 in. (15 cm) clusters of white flowers in late spring, followed by scarlet berries and maroon-purple leaves. The plant has a strongly horizontal habit of growth, which works well in a Japanese-style garden.

*The fruits can cause a mild stomach upset if eaten.*

Facing page: Evergreen varieties of viburnum like this *Viburnum tinus* 'Pink Prelude', flower early in the year when pollinating insects are emerging from hibernation.

### Where to plant

Viburnums generally prefer moderately fertile, moist, well-drained soil and a sunny site. Use singly or in groups of three in a shrub border or woodland edge to create a dense thicket or wildlife-friendly screen. To minimize the risk of powdery mildew, choose a site where air can circulate freely.

### Caring for plants

Established plants are best pruned in summer immediately after they have flowered, when up to one-fifth of the oldest and weakest branches should be cut down to the base. Remove any vertical shoots that threaten to spoil the shape of *V. plicatum* f. *tomentosum* 'Shasta' to their point of origin.

*Note:* Viburnum opulus *is listed as invasive in Wisconsin.*

The spring-flowering *Viburnum* x *juddii* (Zones 4–7) has an outstanding fragrance.

# *Viola tricolor*

## Wild pansy

### Zones 4–9

Wild pansies are wildlife-friendly relatives of the larger brightly colored hybrid pansies that are popular for use in bedding schemes. Over a long period from midspring to early autumn, plants produce a succession of cheerful, five-petaled flowers in shades of violet, lavender, yellow or white, held proudly on slender stems. The caterpillars of several common species of butterfly and moth love to feed on the heart-shaped leaves. Like other species of *Viola*, wild pansies are a favorite with bumblebees and, strange though it may seem, this hefty pollinator can easily straddle the delicate petals to sip the nectar, whereas the overblown blooms of cultivated varieties present great difficulties.

### Where to plant

Wild pansies thrive in moist, well-drained garden soils, although areas where pansies or violets have been grown in the past are best avoided. They are perfect for naturalizing in a wildflower meadow or border, where they will perpetuate year after year by self-seeding.

### Caring for plants

Although pansies will take care of themselves, removing the faded blooms regularly from spring to midsummer will prolong flowering. From late summer on avoid deadheading to allow the plant to self-seed.

The lower petals of wild pansies often have distinctive dark purple markings, giving the appearance of a tiny face.

# A Zone Map of the U.S. and Canada

A plant's winter hardiness is critical in deciding whether it is suitable for your garden. The map below divides the United States and Canada into 11 climatic zones based on average minimum temperatures, as compiled by the U.S. Department of Agriculture. Find your zone and check the zone information in the plant directory to help you choose the plants most likely to flourish in your climate.

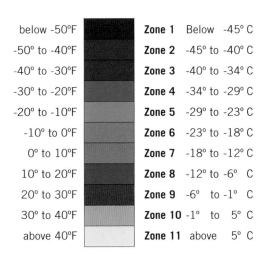

| | | |
|---|---|---|
| below -50°F | | **Zone 1** Below -45° C |
| -50° to -40°F | | **Zone 2** -45° to -40° C |
| -40° to -30°F | | **Zone 3** -40° to -34° C |
| -30° to -20°F | | **Zone 4** -34° to -29° C |
| -20° to -10°F | | **Zone 5** -29° to -23° C |
| -10° to 0°F | | **Zone 6** -23° to -18° C |
| 0° to 10°F | | **Zone 7** -18° to -12° C |
| 10° to 20°F | | **Zone 8** -12° to -6° C |
| 20° to 30°F | | **Zone 9** -6° to -1° C |
| 30° to 40°F | | **Zone 10** -1° to 5° C |
| above 40°F | | **Zone 11** above 5° C |

# INDEX

# ACKNOWLEDGEMENTS

With grateful thanks to Kenneth Creeser whose enthusiasm for wildlife and plants provided the initial inspiration for this book.

The publishers would like to thank Roger Sygrave and Julie Ryan for allowing us to photograph the gardens at Capel Manor College, Middlesex and Roger Platts for allowing us to photograph the plants in his nursery.

Top (t), bottom (b), left (l), right (r).

Pictures on the following pages are copyright ©

**Collins & Brown** 2, 4, 6, 7t, 11l, 12, 17l, 17r, 46, 65, 77, 80, 81, 82, 84, 94, 103, 124, 132.

**Steve Wooster** 1, 7b, 8–9 (Skimmia, Narcissus, Standard Lavender), 10t (The Beth Chatto Gardens), 10b (The Piet Oudolf Borders, Wisley), 11r, 14–15 (Woodstock, South Island, NZ), 16 (Dutch Water Garden, designer: Hank Weyers), 18 (Wollereton Old Hall) 19t, 19b, 20–21 (Priona Garden), 22b, 23b, 26–27 (Green Farm Plants), 28, 29 (all), 30 (all), 32–33 (Bradenham Hall), 35, 36, 37, 38, 39, 40, 41, 42, 43, 44, 45, 48, 49, 50, 51, 52, 53, 54, 55, 56, 57, 58, 61, 62, 63, 64, 67, 68, 69, 70, 72, 73, 74, 75, 76, 78, 79, 83, 85, 86, 87, 88, 90, 92, 93, 95, 96, 97, 98, 99, 100, 101, 102, 106, 107, 108, 109 (Ryton Organic Gardens), 110, 111, 112, 113 (Garden of Riet Brinkhof, Hernen, Holland), 114, 115, 116, 119 (Wisley Garden), 120, 121, 122, 123, 125, 126 (The Beth Chatto Gardens), 127 (The Beth Chatto Gardens), 128, 129, 130, 131, 133, 134, 135, 136, 137 (Yews Farm, Martock), 138, 139, 140.

Photographer in brackets for following:

**Garden Picture Library** 13 (Lynne Brotchie), 23t (Howard Rice), 24 (Janet Sorrell), 25t (Ron Sutherland), 25b (Andrea Jones), 47 (Jerry Pavia), 59 (Ros Wickham), 71 (Chris Burrows), 89 (John Glover), 104 (Howard Rice), 105 (Brian Carter), 118 (Sunniva Harte).

**Holt** 91 (Szadzuck & Zinck).

**Garden World Images** 117 (Incorp. Harry Smith).

**JACKET**
**Front jacket:** David Murray
**Back jacket:** Steve Wooster